Praise for YARN

" '. . . knitting only appears to be a docile activity," writes Kyoko Mori in *Yarn*. While it is knitting that literally and metaphorically weaves together the disparate elements of Mori's life—her travels, her marriage and separation, her coming to knowledge of herself through tragedy and joy—it is the sheer beauty of her writing, at once elegantly restrained and emotionally unflinching, that so highly recommends this stunning memoir. Kyoko Mori is one of the world's most inimitable writers."

—**Howard Norman**, *The Bird Artist* and
What Is Left The Daughter

"Kyoko Mori's books are like red dragonflies at sunset. Afterwards, I'm not sure if I really experienced them or if it was a dream.

Writing as a woman caught between cultures, Mori is a marvelous hybrid of Western realism and Eastern sublimity.

Whether she is remembering her young mother's suicide, a visit with an estranged father, or the return to solitude after marriage, Mori writes with deftness and penetration.

There is no sentimentality in her thoughts, hopes, and memories. Experience seems to fly into the room, like a wounded bird that is nursed diligently.

Even when Mori writes about seemingly banal activities, like a jog along the sea or knitting a sweater, she is trenchant and memorable."

—**Henri Cole**, Lenore Marshall Poetry Prize author of
Middle Earth and *Blackbird and Wolf*

"Kyoko Mori writes about loss so quietly and wisely, and in a way no other memoirist I've read has ever managed. She recasts her mother's suicide and her father's coldness—two terrible childhood absences—into possibilities for herself rather than limitations, openings instead of endings. But this beautiful book isn't about acceptance so much as it's about resourcefulness and creativity. There's no advice here, only the moving example of Mori herself, knitting together her past and present into something coherent and useful, like a shawl, or a cardigan, or a pair of mittens, a way to keep warm in a world that can often be cold, a way to stay focused and engaged in a world that sometimes makes no sense at all."

—**Suzanne Berne**, *The Ghost at the Table*,
A Perfect Arrangement, *A Crime in the Neighbourhood*
(Orange Prize for Fiction), and the forthcoming memoir *Lucile:*
My Grandmother in History, and Vice Versa.

"Sit with Kyoko Mori as she artfully takes in hand needles and fiber, and also the realities of her life story, to knit this gorgeous memoir of loss, emigration, grief, identity and the work of her hands. The perfectly titled *Yarn* recounts the author's most formative experiences, including losing her mother through suicide; emigrating from Japan; finding a life and a love in America's frigid Midwest; discovering joy as a single person; and leaning on the healing power of creating both stories and knitted garments. Scenes and stories become stitches forming a shawl of stories that have draped the author's life, and that will rest so memorably on the shoulders of readers fortunate enough to encounter this book."

—**Suzanne Strempek Shea**, *Sundays in America:*
A Year-Long Roadtrip in Search of Christian Faith

"In *Yarn*, Kyoko Mori employs the metaphor of knitting to devastating effect: strands are wound together seamlessly into a single garment, which is used to keep the wearer/reader/author warm"

— **David Shields**, *The Thing about Life
is that One Day You'll be Dead*

"Save reading Kyoko Mori's *Yarn* for a day when your imagination needs a journey into enchantment. A dreamy weave of memoir and story that is also a droll cross-cultural history of knitting, spinning and weaving, this enthralling, utterly original book is a small masterpiece. I couldn't put it down."

— **Honor Moore**, *The Bishop's Daughter*

yarn

*Remembering
the Way Home*

KYOKO MORI

GEMMA

BOSTON

First published by GemmaMedia in 2010.

GemmaMedia
230 Commercial Street
Boston, MA 02109 USA

www.gemmamedia.com

Printed in the United States of America

14   13   12   11   10   2   3   4   5

978-1-934848-63-0

Library of Congress Control Number:

Parts of this book first appeared in *Harvard Review, The American Scholar, The Missouri Review, Southern Indiana Review* and *The Best American Essays 2004.*

for Jane R. Thompson, Katie Lyons, and Junko Yokota
— thank you for knitting with me over the years

Contents

ONE

Yellow Mittens

THE YELLOW MITTENS I made in seventh-grade home economics proved that I dreamed in color. For the unit on knitting, we were supposed to turn in a perfect pair: two hands held together palm to palm with no extra stitches sticking out from the thumb, the tip of the fingers, or the cuff. Somewhere between making the fourth and the fifth mitten to fulfill this requirement, I dreamed that the ball of yarn in my bag had turned green. Chartreuse, leaf, Granny Smith, lime, neon, acid green. The brightness was electric. I woke up knowing that I was, once again, doomed for a D in home-ec.

I don't remember what possessed me to choose yellow, my least favorite color, for the assignment. In an all-girls school in Japan in 1970, home-ec. was a yearly requirement. Our teacher, Mrs. Amasaki, was a mousy woman with grey hair tucked behind her ears. The previous semester in her class, I had made a skirt with the zipper sewn inside-out, and our cooking team had baked a sponge cake that resembled volcanic rock. But knitting involved no sewing machine to mangle my fingers in, no gas stove to burn down the model kitchen. As I finished one misshapen mitten after another that didn't match, I was surprised by how bad I was.

Mittens, as it turns out, are just about the worst project possible for a beginner. Each hand must be knitted as a tube, with the stitches divided among four pointed needles that twist and slip unless you are holding them with practiced confidence. The pair won't be the same size if you drop or pick up extra stitches along the way, skip a couple of decreases in shaping the top, or knit too tightly in your nervousness and let up in relief as you approach the end. You might make two right mittens or two lefts, because you forgot that the thumb should be placed in a different position for each hand. I ended up with two right hands of roughly the same size and three left hands that could have illustrated a fairytale:

Once upon a time, there lived three brothers, each with only one hand—large, medium, and very small. Even though the villagers laughed at them and called them unkind names, the brothers could do anything when they put their three left hands together.

The perfect mittens a few of my classmates had managed were folded together on Mrs. Amasaki's desk. The girls who'd made them sat near her, working on a second pair with pretty ruffled cuffs. When Mrs. Amasaki got up and walked around the room, I kept my head down. The majority of the class eventually came up with an acceptable pair. Mrs. Amasaki lined up these mittens—not quite perfect—in a separate row on her desk and gave the students an easier project, a scarf, to complete for extra credit.

On the last day of the knitting unit, I had a revelation. One of the two right hands, turned inside-out, became a left hand. I submitted my project with a note explaining the advantage of my design: even in the dark, I could tell the right mitten from the left whose inside-out stitches had tiny bumps like Braille. Mrs. Amasa-ki gave me a D-. At parent-teacher conference, she told my step-mother, Michiko, that I was a smart but undisciplined student. By then, my mother, Takako, had been dead for a year.

UNLIKE MOST JAPANESE COUPLES of their generation, my parents had married for love. They met in 1954 in Kobe at Kawasaki Steel, where Takako was working as a secretary and Hiroshi as an engineer. Her parents opposed the match, because they thought Hiroshi was flashy and arrogant. His parents were lukewarm about my mother as well. Hiroshi's father owned a paint company whose business was prospering, but Takako's family had lost all but a small portion of their land—their main source of income—in the farm reform that followed World War II. Takako and Hiroshi got engaged anyway. Soon after, he was hospitalized with tuberculosis and spent a year in a sanatorium. Takako quit her job and sat by his bedside, working on whatever needlework she could take in to send money to her parents, younger brothers and sisters. She wove ties on a miniature loom, embroidered flow-ers on handkerchiefs, and knitted socks and scarves for a whole-saler. My uncles and aunts would tell me later, Takako was clever with her hands and resourceful: as a young woman, she believed that hard work could reverse any misfortune. After Hiroshi recov-ered, both families relented. "What choice did your grandparents have?" my uncle Shiro said. "Your mother was determined to marry your father. No one could stop her."

Takako must have been remembering the year she'd spent by Hiroshi's bedside with her needlework when she chose "Six Swans," a tale about a knitting princess, for my bedtime story. By then, my parents had been married for five years. I was four, and my brother, Jumpei, a few months old. We still lived in the small house in Kobe where my parents had been newly-weds, but Hiroshi no longer came home every night. While Takako was pregnant with me, he had started seeing another woman.

Once upon a time, the Brothers Grimm story went, a king who had lost his wife was tricked into marrying a witch. Afraid for the safety of his seven children, the king hid them in a forest, but the stepmother found them and turned his six sons into swans. His daughter escaped and wandered through the forest until she discovered the hut where her brothers rested for a few hours at night when they were able to resume their human forms. They told her that the only way to break the spell was to knit a shirt of nettles for each of them; she had to finish the task in seven years, and during that time, she was forbidden to speak or laugh.

A king from another country saw her knitting in the forest, fell in love with her, and married her, but when his jealous mother accused her of being a witch, the girl could not speak to defend herself. The day she was to be burned at the stake was the last day of her seven years' silence. As she was led to the public square, six swans flew out of the sky and landed at her feet. She threw the shirts over them, all but the left sleeve of the smallest one finished. Her brothers turned back into human beings, and the king learned what a devoted sister his wife had been. After a big celebration, everyone lived happily ever after.

Everyone, that is, except the jealous mother-in-law. She was burned at the stake for her lies. Nothing remained of her except a handful of ashes.

IN THE PICTURE BOOK Takako read to me, the princess sat on a grey stone floor in a dimly-lit jail, holding a pair of needles. The balls of yarn at her feet were the dark green of the rose bushes in our garden in winter and, like them, full of thorns. From between the bars on the high window, a sparrow reeled yarn into the room with his beak, and a mouse stood on the floor winding it into a ball. The finished shirts looked scaly, like armor.

My mother was reading this story to keep up her own courage. Like the princess, she had only her hard work and patience to rely on. For seven years, she sat alone with her sewing and embroidery every night after putting Jumpei and me to bed. At one or two in the morning, Hiroshi would call from the bar where he'd been drinking with his friends to say that he was going on a business trip instead of coming home. By the time I was eleven, our family had moved to a large house on a hill in a quiet suburb, and Hiroshi had several girlfriends who telephoned late at night, looking for him. When my mother or I said he was away on business, the women cried and accused us of lying.

Takako covered the walls of our new house with the tapestries on which she'd embroidered rose vines, birds, butterflies, poppies and pansies, boys and girls in red costumes dancing down a tree-lined avenue. She sewed my dresses—my favorite was black velvet with a full skirt and a white lace collar—and designed a special tote bag for each lesson I took. She came to my piano recitals, dance concerts, and watercolor exhibits in the A-line dresses she'd made, her hair cut shoulder length and parted in the middle, her face touched lightly with modest makeup. She was the envy of my friends. "Your mother is so pretty," they said. But in the second winter in the new house, Takako started crying every night. She insisted that Jumpei and I were all she had. If Hiroshi knew how unhappy she was, he didn't show it. On the few days he came home every month, he left early and returned late.

"What will I do when my children are grown? I have wasted my whole life," Takako wrote in the diary she left on the table, next to the dress she was trying to sew for my sixth-grade graduation. She had cut the pieces, pinned them on her sewing board, and then stopped. It was March, 1969, and my mother was forty-one: she couldn't see the point in going on.

⁓

TWO MONTHS LATER, when Michiko moved into our house, Hiroshi said he could have stayed alone with Jumpei and me if I had been more capable. "But you don't know how to cook or clean or take care of your brother," he said, "so I found a woman to keep house for us." Michiko had been one of his girlfriends, of course, but she was determined to stick to his story. To anyone who came to visit, she relished describing how shocked she had been to discover that I didn't know how to use the washer-dryer or the vacuum cleaner. "Her father had warned me," she said with a dry laugh, "but I had no idea any twelve-year-old could be so helpless. Apparently, she'd been raised as a spoiled *Ojosan*."

Ojosan, a rich man's daughter, was what my mother used to be before her family lost their land and she had to go to work as a secretary. Takako must have been relieved when my father became a successful businessman, enabling her to raise my brother and me without worrying about money. Education was more important to her than housewife training. She had read to me, taken me to museums, and signed me up for English, dance, piano, calligraphy, and watercolor lessons.

"I'm sure your friends know how to cook and clean because their mothers showed them when they were little," Michiko said as she smoked a cigarette at the kitchen table. "They'll have nothing to be ashamed of when they meet their future husbands and in-laws. Your mother taught you all the wrong things." Unlike Takako, who'd worn sweaters and slacks around the house, Michiko favored clingy polyester shirts and tight pants in colors like lime green and mustard yellow. Her hair was cut in the pixie style, and even at home, she wore heavy mascara and dark eyeliner like a stage actress.

I didn't bother to tell her that I had helped Takako in the kitchen. I loved separating eggs and dropping only the yolks into a white bowl, dunking tomatoes into boiling water and slipping off the skin under the faucet. For my cousin's birthday, Takako and I had once baked a layered cake that looked like the candy house in Hansel and Gretel, complete with children and a witch cut out of sugar-cookie dough. She showed me how to embroider daisy chains and French knots on silk handkerchiefs. I sewed shirts, skirts, and dresses for my dolls with the backstitch she taught me. Everything we did together was for fun. The stories she told me about my possible future—"When you grow up and go to college," or "If you become a famous author or artist someday,"—never included marriage.

"Maybe you think you'll marry someone who'll let you hire a housekeeper," Michiko said as she stubbed out her cigarette and returned to her daily dusting, mopping, and vacuuming. "No respectable woman pays someone else to clean up after her own family. Too bad your mother didn't train you better. I wish I could teach you, but it's too late." With a rag clenched in her bony fingers, she got down on her knees to peer at the floorboards she had wiped and polished. She was like a witch who believed herself to be Cinderella. "Your father should have disciplined you all along," she said.

Whenever she and Hiroshi quarreled, Michiko blamed me. If Hiroshi hadn't allowed my mother to spoil me, she said, we would all be getting along fine now. She smashed dishes and carried on in a loud voice I could hear all across the house. Soon, she would start packing her suitcase and threatening to leave, and Hiroshi would come tramping upstairs to my room. If I said anything while he was yelling at me, he hit me. If I didn't, he demanded, "Don't you have anything to say for yourself?" He slapped me across the face as soon as I opened my mouth, grabbed me by the shoulders, and threw me against the wall. Then he dragged me downstairs to apologize to Michiko. Hiroshi had never hit me while my mother was alive. Until she died, I had only seen him for a few hours every month. I was relieved when he started staying out again.

By April of 1970—when Michiko came to my school for the parent-teacher conference—my father was out of town half the week. Every night after our supper without him, Michiko swept and scrubbed the kitchen in a fury. Jumpei, now nine, trailed after her. In the months before her suicide, when Takako asked me what I would do if something happened to her and I had to be on my own I'd promised her that I would take good care of myself and Jumpei, that I would be respectful toward Hiroshi and whomever he married so they would treat us well. The only part of the promise I could keep was taking care of myself. Evening after evening, I bolted down my supper and ran upstairs. My bedroom was above the formal drawing room we seldom used. From the large windows next to my bed, I could see the dark reds and sulfur yellows of the sunset. Lying on the mattress above the empty room with furniture covered in white drapes, I tried to imagine my room blasting away from the rest of the house and rising into the sky.

NONE OF MY FRIENDS at school had met my mother. When we started seventh grade, a month after her death, I was the only student in a class of one hundred fifty with just one parent. My classmates gave me worried looks when we read books or sang songs about mothers' love or when our composition teacher asked us to write about our families. There was a girl two classes ahead of us who'd lost her mother in a car crash. Everyone at school, from seventh to twelfth grades, knew who we were—the two motherless girls out of nine hundred. I didn't seek to commiserate with the other girl. More than anything, I was sure, she wanted to be left alone. Besides, even she wouldn't understand.

On the afternoon of my mother's suicide, I had told the police that Takako had been crying for months, that she'd asked me what I would do if she wasn't around anymore. The three officers who came to our house examined the packing tape with which she'd sealed the windows, the gas line she'd unhooked from the stove and held to her mouth, and the diary and the letters she'd left on the table. Then they accepted the money Hiroshi offered and reported her death as an accident. "Think of my children's future," Hiroshi had pleaded. "How could my daughter marry or my son find a job if there was a public record of this?" On the morning of Takako's funeral, Hiroshi told us that our mother had shamed our family. To throw away a perfectly good life—a husband and two children, a comfortable home—was a sign of mental weakness. "Your mother's family was always weak," he said. "You can't see them anymore. Don't tell anyone what happened."

I didn't believe Takako had shamed our family. On the contrary, we had shamed ourselves. I had known for months that she was planning to kill herself. Why else would she ask me to imagine a life without her? And yet everyday when I came home from school and saw her hunched over the kitchen table, I told myself that if I would just listen to her and let her cry, she would soon feel better. While my father was out with his girlfriends, I had sat right next to my mother, refusing to see how desperate she was.

In the letter she left for me, Takako didn't ask me to keep quiet about her death. She said that she loved me, that I should be strong and find happiness without her. I had let her down as surely as Hiroshi had. After making her believe that I, too, would be better off without her, I had failed to speak up when Hiroshi asked the police to lie for us. Then I kept repeating those same lies to everyone, and I had no intention of ever telling the truth.

From time to time, when we were laughing in the school cafeteria or walking around downtown on weekends, my friends could forget about me being the only motherless girl in our class. They chuckled at my jokes, teased me for getting lost at the train station, and scolded me for once again misplacing my wallet or movie ticket. If I told them that my mother had killed herself and my father beat me to please his new wife, all of that would change: my confession would blot out everything anyone ever knew or thought about me. Unlike Hiroshi and Michiko, my friends loved me. They would cry for me and console me the best they could. My mother had chosen to die rather than go on pretending that she was content with her life, but I didn't have the courage to face the truth. If no one knew my secret, then at least when I was away from home, I could continue to act like the spoiled, absent-minded girl I used to be before Takako started crying. I preferred my father's lies to the truth that would single me out forever.

AT OUR SMALL PRIVATE SCHOOL, I had the same classmates year after year, and the dozen close friends I made among them were the rebellious types who wore faded jeans and wrinkled T-shirts to school, hair cut short as a boy's or pulled back into plain, hippie-style ponytails. We were on the cooking teams that burned the sponge cake and the cream puffs and the fancy cupcakes; we turned in our mangled sewing projects and made fun of Mrs. Amasaki.

The only girl I ever saw knitting outside the home-ec. class was Kimiko, a quiet straight-A student who blushed easily. During the winter of our high school sophomore year, Kimiko sat in the back of our classroom during recess, knitting a blue cable sweater for a boy who went to an all-male academy one train stop away from our school. He had asked her out the first time by slipping a note to her as she and her sisters were getting off the train. The oldest of three daughters, Kimiko was supposed to keep her family's name from dying out. When she graduated from college, her parents would arrange a marriage for her with some family's second or third son who could give up his last name to take theirs. She had no future with her boyfriend, who was an only child. Two sisters waited in the reading room of the public library nearby while the pair sat in a coffee shop or walked hand-in-hand on the pier downtown. Then, all three sisters went home together to keep their parents from growing suspicious.

The sweater Kimiko was making had braided cables that looked like totem poles. The patterns were crowded together and the stitches twisted, crossed, and arranged into thick knots. No matter how careful Kimiko and her sisters were, it was only a matter of time before their parents would discover her secret. She had to cram every embellishment she knew into the only garment she would ever knit for that boy.

Kimiko wasn't a close friend, so I was more baffled by her than saddened on her account. I wondered how a girl whose hands and voice trembled in class could disobey her parents for a secret romance while I cowered in my room and listened to my stepmother downstairs baiting my father to hit me. I didn't dare visit my maternal grandparents, uncles, or aunts against Hiroshi's orders, and the secret I was keeping from my friends was bigger than the one Kimiko hid from her parents. I didn't see how that secret would come between my friends and me until it was too late.

DURING OUR FIRST SEMESTER at college, my friends suddenly started skipping our literature classes for the flower arrangement, tea ceremony, French cooking, and pastry-baking lessons with private teachers their parents had hired for their *hanayome shugyo* (bride training). When they did come to school, they were wearing long skirts and frilled blouses instead of the old jeans and T-shirts; their hair was carefully styled to frame their faces. Miya was setting aside a portion of her monthly allowance for the college tuition of the children she planned to have someday. Makko took driving lessons so she could participate in future car pools. Even Sachiko, the biggest tomboy among us, signed up for an afternoon class at the Shiseido counter of a department store to learn how to apply makeup.

None of these girls had seen their parents holding hands or talking affectionately to each other. Like mine, their fathers stayed out late or failed to return home. Everyone in our school came from the same upper-middle-class background. Men and women lived in separate worlds, and marriage was for security. Our future husbands would go out drinking with their work friends and girlfriends while we waited at home, embroidering tapestries and supervising the children's homework. My friends had never had boyfriends, but no one expected them to. Most women of our generation, like our mothers', had arranged marriages.

My own mother had married for love, only to kill herself a month after her forty-first birthday, so I knew my friends wouldn't be any worse off with an arranged marriage than with a love match. Still, I couldn't believe how easily they were going along with their parents' plans for their future. Back in high school, we had often come across families gathered for *omiai*, the formal first "date" toward an arranged marriage, at the hotel lobbies we cut through on our way to the movies. A dozen men and women in their suits and *kimonos* sat uncomfortably together making stilted conversation. Entire families were there—the couple on their first "date," their parents, siblings, aunt, and uncles. "*Omiai*," we whispered and snickered as we walked on.

If we ever had to get married, we'd said to each other, we wouldn't let our parents find us husbands from "a nice family" like ours. On our own, we would choose artists or musicians who had grown up in foreign countries, or in remote northern towns like the "Snow Country" of Kawabata's novel, or in poor struggling families we read about in our social studies classes. Only boys like that were guaranteed to be different from our fathers. But when I reminded my friends of these conversations, they laughed and said I was being childish. Without knowing my secret, they couldn't understand why I was so set against marriage. But I felt betrayed, all the same.

Hiroshi and Michiko didn't encourage me to take up tea ceremony or flower arrangement, but when I turned nineteen, they made a list of acquaintances with sons my age. Perhaps in a few years, they said, one of these families would be interested in having me as their daughter-in-law. Michiko said it was too late for me to learn to keep house the proper way; I was sure to bring shame on our family. When she threatened to leave again one night, I said I would go rent a room. "I'll be the one to leave," I offered. "You can stay." Hiroshi was furious. Young women from good families didn't leave their parents' house except to marry. Any woman living alone was bound to be someone's Nigo-san (Number Two Wife). Since I wasn't allowed to work like a poor man's daughter, I had no money for rent anyway. Hiroshi paid my tuition and gave me a monthly allowance, as did all my friends' parents.

At the end of our sophomore year, I won a two-year scholarship to finish my B. A. at our sister college in Rockford, Illinois. The scholarship included room and board and a job at the library, so I no longer needed Hiroshi's money. My friends came to the airport on the day I left and cried. For once, they understood what I didn't say: I was never coming back.

IN THE NEXT TWO YEARS, while I applied to graduate school to study writing, my friends back home advanced through their long *omiai* process. Their parents reviewed stacks of dossiers gathered by a professional matchmaker or a family friend. Once they found a good prospect, they asked the matchmaker to set up an *omiai* (the word means "mutual-looking") with the young man's family. Some of my friends only had one "date" and others, several, before their families could agree on a match to pursue. Then there was a long period of waiting while each family hired a private investigator to scrutinize the other's background. By then, it was the last semester of college, and my friends could scarcely sleep or eat.

Growing up, we had heard horror stories about marriage proposals that fizzled out when a detective discovered that the prospective bride's aunt had suffered from mental illness or her great-grandfather had been adopted rather than born into the family. Every illness or misfortune was suspected to be hereditary, something a woman could pass on to her children. No family would have wanted their son to marry me if they knew about my mother's suicide. Even after I was married, my husband would have divorced me and disowned any children we had, if he found out. My father expected me to continue his lie as long as I lived, because when a woman failed to find and keep a proper husband, her whole family was disgraced.

Makko wrote a week before her college graduation with the news of her engagement. "All the stress I felt in the last two years is gone," she declared. "The uncertainty is over. Now I can settle into my life." In the fall, others sent me wedding photographs. Each girl wore a traditional Japanese *kimono* for the ceremony, changed into a wedding dress for the reception, and left for her honeymoon dressed in a two-piece suit and pillbox hat like Jackie Kennedy. Their faces made up, their hair professionally styled, these young women looked nearly identical.

By then, I was in graduate school in Milwaukee. My friends stopped writing after they were married, so I don't know whom Kimiko's family chose as her husband and their *yo-shi-san* ("an honorable adopted son.") I imagined her knitting baby socks for her children and wondered if she still remembered the sweater she'd made for her boyfriend, with the raised stitches that crossed over, split apart, and came together again.

I LEARNED TO KNIT in the last year of graduate school from the German Rotary Scholar at our university. Like me, Sabina was short and plain. Her brown hair was cut straight across her nape, and her wire-rimmed glasses gave her eyes a pinched look, but she had a closet full of beautiful sweaters. She came to school in a ruffled mohair shell one week, a sturdy fisherman's pullover the next.

"I make all my sweaters," she said when I complimented her on the red angora cardigan she was wearing. "I can teach you."

I told her about my mitten fiasco.

"Knitting is easy," she insisted. "A sweater is bigger than a mitten but much simpler."

"The pattern will confuse me."

"You don't need patterns. You can make things up as you go."

On the April afternoon I turned in my creative writing dissertation—a manuscript of short stories and poems—the spare bedroom I used as my study looked too tidy. I had thrown out the earlier drafts of everything I'd put into the dissertation, the written comments I'd received from my teachers and fellow students, the notes I'd taken. My desk top was as spotless as my stepmother might have left it.

"Can I still get that knitting lesson?" I called Sabina and asked. "I don't know what to do with my time."

Sabina showed me the only six things I needed to know to knit a sweater: cast on, knit, purl, increase, decrease, cast off. She placed two chairs side by side in the kitchen and sat next to me. To my surprise, I recognized everything she was doing: the yarn wrapped around the palm like a cat's cradle for the cast-on; the row of stitches, the size of rice grains, lined up on the needle; the tip of the other needle going in and sliding more yarn through. I picked up a long bamboo needle—less slippery than the thin metal ones from Mrs. Amasaki's class—and a ball of light blue yarn from Sabina's basket. The first stitch of every garment is a slipknot. I tugged the yarn so the knot was snug but not too tight around the needle and cast on nineteen more stitches. The first row, I remembered, is always the hardest, because there is no fabric yet to hold onto.

"Hey, you're catching on very quickly," Sabina said when a blue square began to form on my needles. "We should walk over to the yarn store so you can get some yarn and start your sweater right away."

The store was on a busy street next to a Chinese restaurant. In the window, a fuzzy pink sweater and a long purple shawl floated on invisible wires. Inside, in a space no larger than my writing room, more sweaters hung from the ceiling, and the walls were lined with plastic milk crates turned on their sides to provide shelving. Balls and skeins of yarn were everywhere—in the crates, in the baskets on the floor, in bags against the wall. Some had swirls of colors like peppermint or taffy. I was inside Hansel and Gretel's candy house made of yarn, with the swans' sweaters flying overhead.

I bought five skeins of red cotton with a nubby texture. Over the next two weeks, following Sabina's instructions, I first made the body of the sweater: two flat pieces, front and back, with simple decreases to shape the shoulders and the neck. They were surprisingly easy to sew together with a large blunt needle, using the backstitch my mother had taught me for my doll's clothes. Sabina showed me how to pick up the stitches along the arm opening, connect the yarn, and knit the sleeves, going from the shoulder to the wrist. I finished my first sweater in a month. The result was slightly lopsided—one sleeve was half an inch wider than the other—but the arms looked even once I put the sweater on. Small mistakes in knitting disappear when the garment is on the body, where it belongs.

I wore the sweater to my dissertation defense at the end of May and to the party afterward. I was twenty-seven, done with my Ph. D., and married to a man from Green Bay, Wisconsin—a small town a hundred miles north where I had gotten a tenure-track teaching job to start in the fall. I could finally learn to knit and catch up on home-making because my life was nothing like my mother's, and my husband was more unconventional than anyone I knew.

BY THE TIME WE MET, halfway through my graduate studies, Chuck had been in college on and off for ten years, changing his major from philosophy to environmental science to visual art, music, general humanities, then psychology. At twenty-seven, he had moved from Green Bay to Milwaukee to finish the elementary education degree, his absolute final choice, and found an apartment with a couple of other students—one of whom was my classmate, George. The early spring night George and I decided to watch the lunar eclipse, we were making coffee and dragging our chairs from the kitchen to the fourth-floor balcony, when Chuck came home from his band practice. As I held the door open for him to carry in his amp, he told me he was the bass player in a wedding band. He said he even sang a couple of songs that weren't right for their female vocalist, like "Blue Eyes Crying in the Rain."

He always forgot the lyrics after the first verse, but people were too drunk to care, so he hummed the tune, implying that the words were too profound to be vocalized.

"I came to see the eclipse with George," I told him.

"Cool," Chuck said. "I'll get another chair."

He put his chair between George's and mine and sat down. The moon looked full but nothing happened for hours. By the time the eclipse started, George was asleep in his chair. As we passed his binoculars back and forth between us, Chuck told me about working on the railroad on the Minnesota border the summer he was eighteen. From a resort town nearby, he'd sent a picture postcard of a Northern Pike, a truly ugly fish, to his girlfriend with whom he was on the outs, with the message, "Thinking of you." He'd hoped she would laugh and write back, but she didn't. When he came back to town, he got a job as a cab driver. On his first night, two drunk women squeezed into the front seat, and one of them tried to kiss him. He dropped them off and called the dispatcher to report, "Number Nine, coming in." The dispatcher replied, "Number Nine, you just started your shift. It's not time for you to come in." "The hell it is," Chuck told him, "because I'm quitting right now."

Chuck was wearing jeans, a black T-shirt, and a denim jacket, with a folded red bandana tied around his forehead like "Easy Rider" outlaws, but his shoulder-length hair, pulled back with a rubber band, curled under on his nape like a little girl's ponytail. With his high cheek bones and long eyelashes, he was just the kind of good-looking guy a drunk woman in a cab might feel safe enough to kiss. When he told me he was studying for a teaching certificate, I couldn't picture him in a classroom. The only young male teacher I'd ever seen was Sidney Poitier in "To Sir, With Love."

"I decided to become a teacher because I never had a good teacher myself," Chuck said. "I want to encourage kids to think for themselves and break the rules."

After George went to bed, the two of us stood on the edge of the balcony howling at the moon as it reappeared. Chuck walked me home, and we made plans to go running the next day. In the fall when he finally asked me out, Chuck told me that he had actually seen me running during his first week in Milwaukee the year before.

"You looked really strong and determined," he said. "I saw you every week after that and wondered who you were and where you lived. I had no idea we actually lived on the same street. I couldn't believe when you were in my apartment talking to George. I almost said, 'Hey, you're the runner I've been wanting to meet for months! I hope you're not planning to date George.'"

For all that, it had taken Chuck nearly six months of our running together every week to ask for a date. "I never wanted to be the kind of guy who moves too fast," he explained. "Whatever was going to happen between us, I figured it just would, if it was meant to be."

Unlike my graduate school friends, who couldn't stop talking about their worst childhood memories, failed poems and romances, Chuck didn't dwell on the past or worry about the future. On the stone wall along the bike path where we ran together, someone had scrawled in red paint, "Those who remember the past are condemned to repeat it." It was Chuck's favorite graffiti. "So true," he said. "Going over all that negative stuff in your mind is how you get trapped into the same bad karma."

The week before Thanksgiving, when Chuck and I had been seeing each other for three months, George announced his intention to find his own apartment, and on that same afternoon, my friend Dale confided that his wife had left him so he could no longer afford his two-bedroom flat.

"You and I can take over Dale's flat and he can have this one," Chuck suggested as we sat drinking coffee at midnight in the basement studio where I had been living with my Siamese attack cat, Dorian. "Things happen for a reason."

"I thought you were moving when you finish school," I pointed out. "That's next month." On the night we first met, Chuck had told me he would apply for a job in Chicago or New York after getting his teaching certificate in December.

"I don't have to do that right away," he said now. "It's not like I've looked into it yet."

I still had two more years of school and had no idea where I would find a teaching job afterward.

"Don't worry about all that stuff yet," he said. "No big deal. It'll all work out. We should try living together for a couple of years. Then we'll see how things go."

He'd had a dozen girlfriends and roommates in the past, but they were never the same people. I had only dated one other person, my senior year in college, long enough to refer to him as my boyfriend. Aside from my family and the two roommates who didn't work out my first summer in Milwaukee, Dorian was the only living being with whom I had ever shared my space. Chuck and I toasted our move-in decision with our coffee, marveling at our spontaneity and saying we would just "play it by ear," whatever *it* was.

A month after we moved in together, Chuck graduated from college at twenty-eight and got a job teaching third grade at a small parochial school. In the world of my childhood, no one who worked on the railroad or drove a cab ever became a teacher. And none of my Japanese friends had lived with anyone unrelated to her by blood or marriage

A YEAR AND THREE MONTHS LATER, when fifty job applications resulted in two offers, I chose a position in Green Bay for its lighter teaching load. I was almost done with my dissertation but nowhere near publishing my first book of stories or poems. My student visa would expire as soon as I finished my degree. I needed a job that would qualify me for a work visa and allow me to continue writing. I accepted the Green Bay job on the phone and called the other college to decline their offer.

I didn't expect Chuck to return to Green Bay anymore than I would to Japan. "I can come back to see you on weekends if you want," I added after telling him the news. He had just returned from work, and we were sitting in our living room on the red velvet couch I had inherited from a poet who'd moved to New York and left me his furniture.

"I'll go with you," he said. "It'll be too weird to have you living in my hometown without me. Besides, it's not like I have a job I can't give up." The parochial school was on the verge of a financial collapse. Teachers had been asked not to cash their paychecks, because there were no funds to cover them, and the heat in the classrooms had to be turned so low that the students sat at their desks in their hats and gloves.

"You could still go to New York, or Italy," I suggested. We had heard on the news that New York City had severe teacher shortage, and a friend had given him a brochure about a Montessori school in Rome.

"Listen," he said, taking my hand, "if someone had told me when I first got here that I was going to meet a woman from Japan who was going to bring me back to live in Green Bay, I'd have said, 'You've got to be kidding me.' But what can I say? This is how things turned out. I still want to go with you."

My job decision had made perfect sense when I was alone, but now, it seemed bizarre. I had applied in every state from Alaska and Hawaii to Maine and Florida and ended up with an offer from Chuck's hometown. We sat in a daze all afternoon until he said, "We have to believe there are no coincidences. Otherwise, this will drive us crazy."

A few days later, when I found out that I would still have to leave the country after defending my dissertation in May and apply for a work visa from Japan, Chuck said we should get married.

"We already made a commitment by moving in together," he said. "So what's the difference?"

That wasn't remotely how I remembered it.

"We didn't make a commitment. We said nothing about the future."

"Maybe not," he shrugged. "Still, you're the first person I ever wanted to live with. I wouldn't have moved in with you if I didn't feel committed."

"But getting married is a big deal. We shouldn't do it just so I can get a visa."

"Why not? It's one of the best reasons I ever heard. Why go through the hassle when we can drive down to city hall?"

According to a counselor I'd gone to see at our university's legal clinic, getting a job offer didn't automatically qualify me for a visa. Work visa applications could take up to a year, and many were turned down. In the meantime, if I didn't leave the country as soon as my student visa expired, I would be deported as an illegal alien and disqualified from every coming back. After all these years, I was going to have to live in Hiroshi's house again and wait for a visa that might never come through. But Chuck had told me about the women he'd dated in Green Bay—how they pressured him about marriage until he couldn't stand to be with them.

"You said you didn't want to get married," I reminded him. "You don't believe in marriage."

"I only said I don't believe in weddings. People act like idiots at weddings. Weddings are phony and stupid."

In the framed photograph of their wedding my mother had kept on her dresser, my parents stood in front of the Heian Shrine in Kyoto: Hiroshi in a black suit, Takako in a rented dress that was too long for her. She had told her parents, "If Hiroshi dies from tuberculosis, I want to be buried with him. I'll never marry anyone else." Standing in that white dress in front of the oldest shrine in Kyoto, Takako couldn't have imagined that a year later, Hiroshi would be having his first affair. Ever since her suicide, I had been determined to avoid her mistake by not getting married, but now, the only way I could escape being sent back to my father's house was to get married.

"We can just go to the court house," Chuck said. "The ceremony is only a formality. We shouldn't make such a big deal out of it."

"But what if things didn't work out between us?" I asked.

"We'll deal with it then," he said, "if it happens that way. There's no guarantee for the future."

I was relieved to hear him say he wasn't making any promises about the future. Getting married was just a formality, something he was willing to do to help me. If Chuck had sworn he loved me for always and wanted to be with me forever, I would have told him the truth. I didn't believe in marriage if it meant vowing to be with anyone for the rest of my life. The only promise I wanted to make about the future was that we would let each other go if things didn't work out, before one or both of us were destroyed by our marriage. But Chuck was already saying the same thing. We could get married because neither of us believed in "till death do us part."

We drove to the court house the next day for our marriage license and had our civil ceremony a few weeks later, telling no one about it until it was over. Finding a job, finishing my dissertation, getting my driver's license after four failed road tests, even learning to knit and cook—I believed these were my real rites of passage.

THAT SUMMER, as Chuck and I prepared for our move, I started a second sweater for myself and read the vegetarian cookbooks from which I had been making a few easy soups, salads, and sandwiches every week. Though I didn't know how, I had volunteered for cooking when the two of us divided our chores, because I preferred it to cleaning and dishwashing. Aside from the sponge cake and fancy cupcakes, our home-ec. classes had taught us to make radish roses and cucumber threads, chocolate soufflés, cream puffs, platters of *tempura*, birds' nest soup. Even if I had been paying attention, I wouldn't have learned how to cook everyday meals for two people.

Because cookbooks were written in numbered sentences without words like *the* and *and*, I'd imagined a tight-lipped, dour woman speaking to me through the recipes, like Mrs. Amasaki and my stepmother combined. I was stunned to discover that the recipes were actually simple and easy. Almost every baking recipe began with "Preheat (the) oven to 350 degrees." For most main dishes, you heated the oil in the pan while cutting the vegetables and measuring the spices. All you had to do was follow a few directions and figure out the rest as you went along.

Like knitting, cooking called for a trial-and-error approach. The first curry recipe I made said, "Add a quarter cup of water or more, as needed, to prevent burning and sticking." Every soup, pasta sauce, or casserole recipe advised, "Season to taste." In knitting, if the sweater was turning out too large or too small, I could throw in extra decreases or increases to adjust the size. I could unravel the yarn on purpose, undo a few inches of work, and correct my mistakes. Best of all, if the finished sweater was half an inch too small, it would always stretch.

No one cared if their mittens were exactly the same size, any more than if the radish rose on their plate was missing a petal. Knitting and cooking were different from sewing. Before you even threaded your needle to sew, you could have made an irreversible mistake by cutting the pieces wrong; then you'd have to buy more cloth and lay out the pattern again. Every time you rip out stitches because you sewed the wrong parts together, the cloth frays. If the finished shirt is half an inch too small, it's not going to stretch.

The words *thread* (the string-like material we sew with) and *yarn* (the string-like material we knit with) convey different degrees of flexibility. Thread holds together and restricts, while yarn stretches and gives. Thread is the overall theme that gives meaning to our words and thoughts—to lose the thread is to be incoherent or inattentive. A yarn is a long, pointless, amusing story whose facts have been exaggerated. I had gotten D's in home-ec., math, and science because I was concocting a yarn in my head when I should have been following the thread of each lesson.

Thread was all I got at home after my mother's death. Every time my stepmother said I would disgrace our family when I married because my mother hadn't taught me the right skills, she was talking like a sewing teacher: I had made a mistake, I couldn't fix it, and I only deserved a D. Michiko was saying what everyone around us believed. In Japan, a woman had one chance for a secure marriage. My mother couldn't reverse the mistake she'd made by choosing the flashy, arrogant man her parents had warned against. If she had left Hiroshi, she would have lost my brother and me— like everything else in our parents' house, we belonged to Hiroshi and not to Takako—and even the people who knew about Hiroshi's affairs would have blamed her. She had nowhere to go except back to her parents' house to become a financial burden. Takako was like a seamstress who had ruined the only piece of cloth she was given. She didn't get a second chance for happiness. She dreamed of me becoming a writer or an artist so I would have the freedom she never knew.

But if she'd ever envisioned me getting married, she might have chosen someone like Chuck, a teacher who encouraged his students to think for themselves and break the rules. Chuck would never cheat on me and lie to me as my father had done to my mother. Even more important, he valued freedom and open-mindedness as much as he did honesty. If we became so miserable together that one of us wished to die, he, too, would want us to go our separate ways to be happy alone or with someone else. In the meantime, as long as we both chose, ours could be a marriage of yarn: two flexible strands connected loosely into a warm sweater, a good story instead of a terrible lesson.

I DIDN'T KNOW, THEN, that knitting is a relatively new invention. The oldest surviving knitted objects—blue and white cotton socks discovered in an Egyptian tomb—are dated 1200 A. D., eight thousand years after the first artifacts of weaving: clay balls with imprints of textiles found in Iraq. Weavers appear on papyruses from ancient Egypt and in stories from ancient Greece. In Odysseus' absence, Penelope weaves and unweaves a funeral tapestry for her father-in-law to keep her suitors away. Arachne is turned into a spider when she challenges the goddess Athene to a weaving contest and loses. No Greek hero's wife or foolish mortal ever received praise or punishment for knitting. The earliest images of the craft are from the fourteenth century, when Italian and German artists painted the Virgin Mary knitting in brightly-lit drawing rooms with the baby Jesus at her feet.

A knitted garment, whose loose construction traps air against the body, is warmer but more fragile than a woven one. One broken stitch can release all the others, making the fabric "run." Knitting didn't appear until the middle ages, because the earlier people had no use for fragile luxury goods. The delicate silk stockings knitted in France in the sixteenth century were reserved for the royalty and were more like today's designer shoes than the humble wool socks. Queen Elizabeth I refused to wear the stiff woven-and-sewn socks from her own country after trying on her first pair of soft knitted French silk stockings. Her cousin and enemy, Mary the Queen of Scotts, wore blue-and-gold knitted silk stockings to her execution.

Even in the nineteenth century, when the craft was widespread among the common people, knitted garments were treasured as family heirlooms. Every girl in Latvia learned by the age of six so she could get an early start on mittens for her dowry chest. A full dowry chest reduced the number of cows and sheep her family was required to pay the groom. On the wedding day, the mittens, which had colorful interlocking geometrical designs, were distributed to all the participants from the carriage driver to the minister, to the numerous relatives, in-laws, and neighbors. At the feast, the bride and groom ate with mittened hands to invite good luck. When the day was over, the bride walked around the inside and outside of her new home, laying mittens on all the important locations: the hearth, the doors, the windows, the cow barn, the sheep shed, the beehives, the garden. Depending on the number of guests, she needed a hundred or two hundred pairs of mittens to get through her wedding day.

Knitting with two or more colors makes a stronger fabric than using only one. The tiny diamonds, crosses, squares, and x's and o's repeated across the mittens were proof of the bride's ability to perform the careful, monotonous work of a farm wife. If you held a Latvian mitten up to a lamp, no light would shine through the tightly-packed stitches. Unlike the silk stockings from France, these mittens were as sturdy as any knitted item could be. They were result of many years of labor by the bride who gave herself to her community and her new family, grafting her childhood on to her adult life, marrying her past to her future with the groom. Mittens brought together all the people who received them. The last pairs left were collected by her mother-in-law. Her dowry box finally empty, the bride placed herself under the older woman's guidance, under her thumb.

Knitting was a new craft in Latvia compared to weaving and embroidery, but its purpose was ancient: bringing people together and creating lasting ties. A Latvian wedding was not so different from my friends' *omiai* in hotel lobbies, attended by the families on both sides. A bride secured her family and her community around her by placing herself firmly in the center. She stayed home while her husband went to work. No matter where he'd been or how long (or with whom), he would find his wife caring for their children and guarding their home when he returned. It's an age-old story, from Penelope to my mother to my friends, Makko and Miya. In Japan, the ideogram for safety is a woman under the roof, and a man refers to his wife as *ka-nai*, "house-inside."

THE CIVIL CEREMONY CHUCK AND I had was the opposite of the Latvian wedding. We invited none of our families, relatives, neighbors, or friends our age. Aside from the two of us and the judge, the only people present were Ed and Vicki, a couple in their forties who served as our witnesses. They ran an alternative poetry press; I had met them through my writing, and Chuck scarcely knew them. They home-schooled their teen-age daughter, arguing that they were Zen Buddhists entitled to exercise their freedom of religion. Fifteen years earlier, their own wedding had consisted of driving three times around the water tower in Kenosha, Vicki's hometown. They were supposed to go to the court house afterward but never made it, so their marriage was not recognized by law. We couldn't have chosen two people with fewer ties to the community or to our past.

Chuck and I showed up in our jeans and T-shirts; Ed and Vicki didn't own any other kinds of clothes. When the judge arrived, the ceremony in the living room took five minutes, made even shorter by our omission of wedding rings which we scorned as outdated symbols of oppression ("like a dog collar around the finger," Chuck said). Our wedding day was March 17, 1984. The day before, March 16, had been the fifteenth anniversary of my mother's death, but I said nothing to Chuck. That day was sacred between Takako and me: every year, I took a long walk to think about her and promise her that my life would be different from hers.

As I stood before the judge with Chuck, the only thing I wanted to be tied to was my mother's memory. I kept the family name she had taken at her wedding. Takako had told her parents that she would rather die than live without Hiroshi, but the words Chuck and I repeated only said that we would always love, respect, and honor each other—which we could do even if we were no longer married to each other someday. Takako was my mother forever; Chuck would be my husband as long as he and I chose.

I believed my freedom depended on being able to live my mother's life in reverse. I didn't understand that rebelling against every tradition bound me tighter to my own history. While the Latvian bride opened her dowry box to give away the entire contents of her past, I held onto mine like a mismatched mitten.

Hats

W HILE THE FRENCH WERE knitting silk stockings for the royalty in the sixteenth century, English and Welsh artisans made skullcaps for their soldiers to wear under their helmets. The caps were knitted in coarse brown wool and washed in boiling water until they shrank and turned into felt. In *Henry V*, Shakespeare described the Welsh soldiers at Agincourt wearing leeks in their caps to express their national pride.

The English literature I studied in college was hardy like the soldiers' caps. My favorite Shakespearean hero, Hamlet, pretended to be crazy while he pursued an elaborate plot to make sure that his uncle was guilty of his father's murder. Like anyone who recoils from confrontation, he vacillated between being overcautious and rash. After he stabbed Ophelia's father by mistake, she went mad and drowned, her brother joined the plot to kill him and died by his own sword, and his mother drank from the poisoned cup meant for him. If Hamlet had killed his uncle right away without thinking so much about it, no one else would have had to die, but the revenge he botched showed his humanity.

The classical Japanese literature I'd been taught was tame in comparison. In each chapter our high school class had read from *The Tale of Genji*, a new woman fell in love with our hero and waited all day for his visit, only to receive a seasonal token—a pressed flower, red maple leaves, grass blades tied with silk—and a poem he wrote to apologize for his absence. Though Genji had many lovers, he pined for his stepmother, the one woman he could never marry. No matter how callously he treated the others, he didn't lose his reputation as "the shining prince." Exiled from court, he stood on a deserted beach and shed a few tasteful tears while his followers praised his beauty.

The Tale of Genji was too pretty for me, delicate like the silk stockings reserved for the royalty. I preferred the literature of coarse wool caps, stories about people who said and did terrible things and regretted their mistakes.

THE FIRST HAT I MADE WAS a watchcap, with the same round shape as the soldiers' skullcaps. It started with a band around the forehead. A series of gradual decreases shaped the crown; at the end, I pulled the yarn through the few stitches left on the needles and decorated the top with a pompon. Over the next few years, I knitted a watchcap to match every sweater I made. Depending on the yarn, the caps turned out so sturdy they stood on their own like tea cozies or so fine I could stuff them in my coat pocket.

My friends marveled at the tiny stitches on the finer hats and exclaimed, "You must be so patient." But doing the same thing over and over didn't require any patience; the worst I could be alone was bored. The real test of patience was putting up with other people.

On a family vacation he and Michiko planned the first summer they were married, my father screamed at a man who cut in front of us in the ticket line at the train station. Hiroshi was shorter than average, but he had thick eyebrows and big eyes that flashed out his anger. Even after the offender slouched toward him and mumbled an apology, Hiroshi didn't let up. His face got redder and redder, and he was jumping up and down like an angry little dog. When people started staring at us, I walked away and stood behind a pillar.

I've never yelled at anyone in anger. Whether a repair person shows up in the mid-afternoon for our morning appointment or a friend calls the restaurant where I'm already seated to say she's not coming, my response is always, "Don't worry. I hope everything's okay with you." There is a huge difference between being late and being inconsiderate, between what I should accept from a repair person I will never see again and a friend who should know better. The closer I am to someone, the more important it is to tell the truth. I wish I could emulate the literature I love—the rough edges, the complex emotions, the honesty—but as my impatience flares into anger, I act calmer by the second. With a big false smile, I'll insist there's no problem. I'm worse than *The Tale of Genji*. The words I offer are as brittle as dried grasses tied in silk.

If I let my anger show, what's to stop me from being as out of control as my father, who yelled at people and hit me at home? With Chuck, who didn't like to fight, it was especially easy to remain patient. When he made sarcastic remarks about my friends or came home late while I waited for him to go somewhere with me, I seldom knew how upset I was until hours later when I was alone. By the time we were together again, it seemed petty and embarrassing to bring up an offense he might have forgotten about. Whatever I was upset about, I told myself, it couldn't have been that important if I didn't notice right away. Because my father had no patience, I became patient to a fault. If Hiroshi was fire, then I would be a glacier.

WHEN I FINALLY GOT TIRED of making watchcaps, I started knitting brimmed hats from variegated mohair yarn. The first, finished in two days, looked like a tie-dye-draped lamp shade from a 1960s dorm room. The crown was a purple and pink swirl that covered my face down to the chin, and the brim draped over my shoulders. I threw this enormous hat in the washer set on hot wash and cold rinse and ran the cycle twice. The hat came out shrunken and matted: the stitches had contracted till they were invisible, leaving a dense, fuzzy nap. Like the medieval soldiers' caps, my hat had turned into felt. I reshaped it on a mixing bowl about the size of my head, and by the time it dried, it resembled a professionally made bowler. The lava-lamp swirls had settled into flecked tweed. I knitted a dozen more in different colors and decorated them with beads and embroidery. The felted bowler became a staple of my gift giving, something to knit every fall in anticipation of Christmas.

One November Saturday after I'd moved to Green Bay, I went to an antique mall in Northern Wisconsin with a couple who had fallen in love with an oak dresser. Every weekend for two months, Dan and Lucy had brought a different friend to look at the dresser, to ooh and aah over it, so they could work up the nerve to spend the money. The antique mall was a huge place out in the country crammed with furniture and knick-knacks. When we finally got to the right section, I didn't even notice the dresser because to the right of it, on a shabby card table, stood a wooden hat form. To an untrained eye, the hat form looked like a wooden head, but I knew what it was. Tired of reshaping hats over a bowl, I had been trying to order one, except the modern versions were made of Styrofoam, and I did-n't think I could stand the squeaky noise they would make. I grabbed the wooden head and walked around with it tightly clutched under my arm while Dan and Lucy showed me all the other oak dressers in the entire mall, everyone of them inferior to the one they wanted. When we were through, Dan said, "We should wait." "Yeah, we want to be sure," Lucy agreed, her lips pursed.

I was the worst person to bring to the antique mall. Chuck and I found furniture shopping so overwhelming we just waited for people to give us their hand-me-downs. Our friends and his relatives made our decorating decisions for us by giving us a red velvet couch or a green dining table or a set of white chairs. Nothing matched, and it was impossible to buy a new item to add to the existing mishmash. The only piece of furniture we got on our own—an end table from a rummage sale—didn't fit. "I don't know what more we could have done," Chuck said. He'd gone home to measure the space while I waited at the sale; he'd scribbled the numbers on a piece of paper and brought it back. Later, we couldn't find the paper to see if he'd mismeasured the space or the table or both. Watching Dan and Lucy at the antique mall, I understood that our problem wasn't with the measuring tape.

Lucy sewed, sold, and rented out vintage costumes. Dan ran a dog-grooming business. Each had furnished their work space and made important business decisions and yet—together—they couldn't buy the dresser they both liked. They kept coming back week after week, hoping that whoever they'd brought along would say, "Just buy the dresser and get it over with," or "The dresser's too expensive. You should forget about it."

Being a couple was debilitating. Every time you were faced with a major decision, you mumbled one vague remark after another and waited for your partner to take charge: if something went wrong, then, it would be his fault, not yours. But he had thought of this, too, so the two of you were forever stuck saying, "Really, I don't care. You decide," "No, no, I'm sure you know more about it than I do." "One is the loneliest number," a popular song of our youth declared, but one was the only number that forced us to be decisive.

After we retraced our steps and got back to the counter, I paid twelve dollars for my hat form. It was heavy and compact: a single, powerful head.

⁓

THE WATCHCAP and the felted bowler would have made an ideal two-part project for my home-ec. class. They were the perfect size: small enough not to be intimidating, large enough to hold comfortably in our hands. Mrs. Amasaki must have chosen the mittens because they made us practice the basic techniques at least twice. Repetition is key to learning a new skill, but unlike magic spells, knitting repetition doesn't have to be exact. If a beginner made a watchcap and a felted bowler, she would get plenty of practice with the yarn, the needles, and—as a bonus—the washing machine. Whether you use a modern-day washer or a tub of boiling water and a stirring stick, wool turns into felt when the microscopic scales on its surface are loosened and softened by moisture and heat, then locked together under friction and pressure. To felt a knitted fabric, you do everything you ordinarily shouldn't with wool: wash in extremely hot water with strong soap; spin, rub, roll, and agitate; rinse in cold water; repeat. Shrinking our hats on purpose would have been an unforgettable demonstration. No budding homemaker would have tossed her angora cardigan in hot water afterward.

Mrs. Amasaki must not have known about the wedding mittens of Latvia. If she had, she would have made them an important part of our lesson and examined us on the particulars ("How many pairs of mittens did an average bride knit? A: five; B: fifty; C: two hundred; D: none of the above") since the purpose of our class was to prepare us for marriage. In addition to needlework and cooking, we learned how to plan monthly budgets for a family of four with two children, how to wash, fold, and store various seldom-worn clothes like the husband's tuxedo and the children's New Year's *kimonos*, how to prepare nutritious and attractive lunches for them to take to work and to school. The books Mrs. Amasaki assigned didn't mention single women making a home for themselves or married women having a job outside the home.

Our home-ec. class could have included information about women who'd chosen not to become wives or mothers. Even in the 1970s, there were Japanese women in public life—politicians and educators—almost all of whom were single or married-but-childless. We could have found out if the married career women shared household duties with their husbands, how many of the single women had their own homes and how many lived with their parents, and if these women wished they had husbands and children. We might have read profiles of politicians like Takako Doi, who had gone to high school with my mother. She had been elected to the House of Representatives from Kobe and would go on to become the head of the Social Democratic Party. Many of our own teachers were single. They could have told us what home-making meant to them.

We would have discovered that being single was hard. The majority of the successful single women had parents who were rich, powerful, and unconventional enough to support them. Still, few had their own houses or apartments because—as my father said—women from "good families" did not live alone. Most remained in their childhood homes into their fifties and sixties, cared for their parents, and lived alone only when they themselves were old enough to have been widowed, had they been married. Knowing these things, my friends would have appreciated their marriages more in the future, like the homemaker who—having seen what hot water did to wool—treated her sweaters with extra care.

I would not have married in Japan. After my mother's suicide and the lies my father told about it, I knew that marrying into a Japanese family meant keeping a lifelong secret about Takako's death. My friends' path and mine would have remained separate. Only, I wouldn't have felt so excluded, as though the choices I planned to make were not worth mentioning.

⌒

A MISMATCHED PAIR OF HATS—a watchcap and a bowler—was how Chuck and I wanted to be as a couple. We hated being considered a match, as though one of us, alone, was incomplete. We emphasized our differences even though we only disagreed about one serious topic.

Aside from running, Zen meditation was the only thing Chuck was disciplined about. He meditated every afternoon when he came home from teaching. He had read Alan Watts and D. T. Suzuki and listened to meditation tapes and Zen lecture tapes since he was in high school. None of my Japanese friends had ever studied Zen. The only Buddhism I knew as a child was the "remembering the family dead" variety practiced by most Japanese families, and even that was perfunctory. After my mother's death, my father got an altar for her spirit and stuck it in the room that used to be hers. In the first year after her death, he hired a priest to come to our house to perform the monthly incense burning and sutra reading and invited our neighbors and his coworkers to see what a devoted husband he had been. Because the priest intoned the sutras in the traditional chanting style, his voice alternating between the nasal and the guttural, I had no idea what he was saying. If my mother's spirit was still around, I was sure she wouldn't appreciate being addressed with such an ugly voice.

Hiroshi didn't marry Michiko until the one-year Buddhist mourning period was over, but she had arrived at our house with her red bridal futon two months after Takako's death and moved into his room. When the priest came, Hiroshi didn't invite my mother's parents even though they were the only devout Buddhists we knew. Our neighbors and his coworkers didn't really believe that Takako's spirit was traveling in the land of the dead, in search of our ancestors. When the year was over and the priest came to mark the end of her journey, only my grandparents would have been consoled by the ceremony.

Chuck's parents had signed him up for Confirmation classes in their Lutheran church when he turned fifteen. Every week, his mother dropped him off in the parking lot but Chuck walked through the church, slipped out the back, and ran to the nearby pinball arcade where his friends hung out. One afternoon, a boy with a juvenile record stopped at the arcade in a

stolen car, and Chuck went for a ride with him. On the highway, shortly after Chuck tossed a box of fish tackles out the window to make room for his legs, they were pulled over by a police
officer. "I skipped out of Confirmation to ride around in a stolen
car," was how Chuck summed up his religious education.

Around the same time, I was singing hymns and memorizing Bible verses at our all-girls school, which had been founded
in 1871 by a missionary from Illinois. To leave her home to
teach young Japanese girls in the first few years the country
became open to foreigners after Commodore Perry's arrival, our
founder must have believed as strongly in women's education as
in Christianity. Mrs. Amasaki was an exception. Most of our
teachers were single women from Christian families. Their
fathers had protested World War II and gone to jail; their mothers taught Sunday School and led women's volunteer circles to
help the poor.

Most Christian families in Japan belonged to the educated
upper-middle class. Our parents had sent us to the school
because it was an expensive private academy that specialized in
bilingual education; if they'd known our teachers' political
views, they might have reconsidered. The Christian women
reminded us that Jesus had befriended the outcasts of his society. They criticized our government's treatment of Korean immigrants, its tolerance of businesses that poisoned our waterways. I
went to church every Sunday until I was nineteen, hoping to
believe in the God who inspired my teachers to be so outspoken.
In the end, I couldn't accept that a man who was crucified two
thousand years ago could come back to life and be among us as
our "personal savior." Still, it was a story I wished had been true.

Chuck and I loved arguing about religion. "How could you
believe all that Christian bullshit even if you were so young?"
he would ask, and I would point out that Buddhism, too, had
been used the world over to trick the poor into accepting their
lot. We talked for hours, but our debate only revolved around

the ideas we had acquired as adults. Nothing we said revealed the confused children and lonely teenagers we had once been.

In Japan, less than 1% of the population is Christian—about the same as the minority who practiced Zen Buddhism in Green Bay. Chuck's Zen and my Christianity were one and the same. By the time we were in high school, neither of us was close to our family and we felt misunderstood even by our best friends. In our frustration, we longed for a spiritual practice to set us apart. If we couldn't be understood and appreciated, we wanted to be different, at least, by choice. Chuck had stuck to his beliefs and I had given up on mine, but we were opposites and yet the same, like the right mitten and the left mitten. If we'd been more honest, we could have grown closer.

– TWO –

Seamless Sweaters

A FTER LEARNING TO READ RECIPES, I should have
been able to knit from the pattern books published by yarn
companies. They began with a list of yarns, needles, and notions
like the ingredients and the utensils, and the numbered directions,
such as "Cast on 120 stitches," were similar to "Preheat (the) oven
to 350 F° or "Heat 1 Tbsp of oil in (the) pan." But knitting patterns
also included diagrams like those for assembling furniture and
appliances. A mis-assembled sweater wouldn't surround itself with
smoke and sputter out like the vacuum cleaner I took apart to
clean and put back together (or so I thought); no matter what I did
wrong, there would be no melted electrical cord dangling from
the outlet. Still, those diagrams gave me a headache. I especially
hated the broken lines that meant something should go under
something else. It was unfair to have to follow such complicated
directions only to make a sweater that looked exactly like the photograph on the cover. After all that trouble, a knitter should end
up with an utterly unique garment.

I preferred the way Sabina had taught me to knit by taking my
own measurements and "making things up as you go." My sweater

could be as long or short as I chose; I could use whatever yarn I liked, knit it at the gauge that suited me, and change colors or put in stripes or make the neck extra snug to keep my throat warm. After Sabina went back to Germany, I visited the yarn store by myself and found a book that improved on her method. Instead of making the front and the back separately and sewing them, *The Sweater Workshop* showed how to design a seamless sweater by making three simple tubes (one for the body, two for the sleeves) and knitting them together at the yoke. Once you mastered the prototype seamless sweater—a basic pullover with a crew neck—you could try a v-neck or turtle-neck or add a hood or a pocket or a belt. Each sweater could be as long, short, wide, or narrow as you wanted. Just like in Sabina's method, you chose the yarn, took your own measurements, and "made things up" as you knitted along.

The author, Jacqueline Fee, said she was offering "a retreat from dependence upon others, an alternative for you who wish to knit sweaters on your own, to become an independent, *thinking* knitter." The book was published in 1983, but the oatmeal-colored pullover on the cover had the homespun look of the 1960s back-to-nature movement. Seamless sweaters almost shaped themselves as they grew. Their invisible construction, at once clever and mysterious, made them sturdier than the pieced-together kind. These sweaters were unique without being flashy.

IN GRADUATE SCHOOL, I did nothing but study and run, so I only met other students, teachers, and runners. Moving to Green Bay at twenty-seven, I looked forward to becoming a part of the larger community. I was finally an adult with a real job, and I expected my new life to be as roomy and comfortable as a seamless sweater.

I hadn't considered how different Green Bay was from Milwaukee's East Side. According to the 1980 census, 97% of Green Bay's 87,899 residents were white; among the remaining 3%, only 369 people were of Asian descent, 47 of them Japanese. Milwaukee's population of 636,212 was just 72 % white, and there were 3,459 Asians — 446 Japanese. I didn't exactly blend in anywhere in Wisconsin, but Green Bay was the first place where cars slowed down and drivers turned their heads to stare at me on my morning run. Instead of becoming a seamless part of the community, I stuck out like a lone sweater on a rack of swimsuits. Strangers stopped me in grocery stores and offered to introduce me to the 47 Japanese people in town. "You must be homesick," they said. "I know a Japanese woman who goes to our church. She has an American husband." When I suggested, "Maybe the Japanese woman is an American, too," I got a puzzled smile in response, as though I had recited a Zen koan ("What was your face before you were born?").

Chuck and I rented a two-bedroom apartment in the heart of downtown where the streets were named after trees and presidents, but the area was deserted after the shopping mall on Adams and Cedar closed for the day. Sirens sounded through the night, announcing the shift changes at the Proctor & Gamble paper mill a few miles to the north. "It's like someone dropped a neutron bomb in the middle of the city," Chuck said.

Our apartment was upstairs from a realty office in a small frame house. We had our own side entrance and a rickety stairway leading up to our door. In the eat-in kitchen, the yellow linoleum floor and the lime green curtains matched the old avocado-colored dining table Chuck's parents had passed on to us. Chuck hadn't eaten off that table since two days after his high school graduation in 1972, when he moved out of his parents' house to live with friends in an apartment across town.

In addition to skipping his Confirmation class to ride in a stolen car, Chuck had painted his neighbor's siding with tar on Halloween, stolen beer from garages, shoplifted books and records all over town, built a huge barricade of picnic tables in a park into which a police officer crashed his cruiser and broke his collar bone, and thrown rocks at Richard Nixon's motorcade on its way to the airport. "My parents didn't know what to do with me," he said. "They were relieved to see me move out. My parents are like vanilla—boring but harmless."

I had only met Chuck's parents at family gatherings in crowded restaurants and noisy backyards. His extended family seemed a little bland, but no one really believes that their parents are boring or harmless. Chuck didn't spend his teenage years acting like a juvenile delinquent to protest against vanilla. If I got to know his family better, I thought, I would feel more at home in my new town.

Chuck's parents and grandparents showed up for dinner in their jeans and sweatshirts and sat in our kitchen, carefully passing food around the old table. Chuck's grandfather, Charley Brock, had played football with the Green Bay Packers from 1939 to 1947. Every football season, the pre-game "History of the Packers" program showed pictures of Charley, but unlike the players who came after him, Charley didn't make a lot of money playing football. He and his wife lived in a modest ranch house near Chuck's parents. Dick, Chuck's father, taught social studies at a middle school and had been the star of his high school football team. Chuck didn't play sports when he attended the same high school eighteen years later, because making the team would have required a haircut. Like anyone from Green Bay, however, he watched the Packers every Sunday.

During dinner, while the men talked about football, the women complimented me on the meatless "meatballs" I served over pasta. Chuck's grandmother, Alice, had a wide, pleasant face and wavy white hair parted in the middle. Chuck's mother, Mary, was a slightly overweight woman with platinum blond hair; in her youth, she had looked like Donna Reed. Mary's family was Norwegian, and Alice was from Sweden. Chuck's grandmothers had immigrated to the U. S. as young girls, but no one asked me about growing up in Japan. Unlike the people who stopped me at grocery stores, my in-laws went out of their way not to call attention to my being a foreigner. I wished my new family didn't try so hard to ignore our difference, but I had no idea how to tell them that their politeness was only making me more uncomfortable, so I kept smiling and offering more food.

Charley helped me wash the dishes while the others went to sit in the living room. All I knew about football was that—unlike in basketball—only one person, the quarterback, was allowed to throw the ball. Thankfully, Charley seemed perfectly content not to talk.

After the family left, Chuck said, "Well, that was okay. Everyone seemed to have a good time."

"I guess so," was all I could say.

Dick and Mary were eighteen when Chuck was born. They had three more kids by the time Dick finished college and got his first job as a car salesman. Years later, he went back to school for a teaching certificate. Teaching was a job to Chuck's father, not a calling.

"When I was growing up, my parents didn't have any books," Chuck said. "I never saw them reading. They were too overwhelmed to be great parents, but they did their best. I liked how busy they were. They left me alone. I could do my own thing while they were fussing over the other kids."

In his most recent letter, my father had said I should have studied the literature of my own country before getting a Ph.D. in

English. Michiko said I was lucky to have married a foreigner since no Japanese man would want a wife who was more interested in her studies than in housekeeping. I wrote to them only once every two or three years, because whenever I heard back from them, it took me months to recover from feeling so bad. I couldn't imagine ever having Hiroshi and Michiko over to dinner. The distant but cordial relationship Chuck had with his parents seemed ideal. I didn't understand how lonely Chuck must have felt before he learned to act so independent.

ONE OF THE FRIENDS CHUCK had left home to room with still lived in the country schoolhouse they bought by pooling their money in their early twenties. Chuck, Dean, Dean's brothers, and various friends and their dogs had camped out on the floor of the one room while they renovated the rest of the house. Dean eventually bought out everyone's share, got married, and started making furniture in the wood shop he set up in the basement. Every Saturday, Chuck and I drove out to visit Dean and his wife, Katie.

Katie and I sat upstairs with our yarn and needles while our husbands played guitars in the basement. Katie, a registered nurse, had learned to knit from a neighbor a few years earlier. Like me, she avoided regular patterns and favored seamless sweaters made from three tubes. Designs that required assembling four flat pieces were more versatile if you wanted dropped shoulders, dolman sleeves, fitted bust lines, cinched waists, and other feminine touches, but Katie and I preferred our clothes to be unisex. The seamless sweater, with its rugged raglan sleeves, went well with our baggy jeans, corduroys, and sweat pants.

Katie had a round face, short brown hair, and fair skin; she looked like the portrait of Renoir's wife in the country with a straw hat. Aside from a couple of inches in height, I looked the same as

I had in the seventh grade, with my hair pulled back into a scraggly ponytail. People in Green Bay described me as "tiny," but in Japan, I would have been average height and weight, as Katie was in Wisconsin. Neither of us wore makeup or jewelry, and never wedding rings. We were proud to look healthy and plain.

Katie and Dean had conceded to a church wedding for their Catholic families. In the photograph of the wedding party on their kitchen wall, everyone except Katie, in a white dress but no veil, wore jeans and a peasant shirt, making the group look like a large folk-rock band with a female vocalist. At the ceremony, Katie's brother Tommie had opened the missal on the wrong page and read the passage meant for novices joining the nunnery. Even Chuck, who had grown up Lutheran, knew something was wrong when he heard, "Seven virgins they went into the cave, and seven virgins they came out." Tommie kept reading faster and faster. When he finished, the ceremony went on as though nothing unusual had happened. At the reception, a potluck in the backyard of the schoolhouse, some of Dean's friends clinked the coffee cups with their spoons to make the bride and the groom kiss. Katie stood up alone and announced, "This is the one and only time we're going to do this. I'm not joking. I really mean it." Dean got up, they kissed, and both sat down. No one clinked their cups after that.

Katie had made her first seamless sweater from *Knitting Without Tears* by Elizabeth Zimmermann. Born in 1910 in England, Elizabeth Zimmermann attended art schools in Switzerland and Germany, married a brewer she met in Munich, and immigrated with him to the United States. She started her own knitting newsletters, because she was frustrated by the magazine editors who turned her easy, conversational instructions into obscure jargon that only experienced knitters could understand. She wrote four books, launched a mail-order business of patterns and supplies, hosted a public television show called "The Busy Knitter," and held knitting camps in Pittsville, Wisconsin, where she and her family—like Dean and Katie—lived in a renovated schoolhouse.

"Properly practiced, knitting soothes the troubled spirit," she declared, "and it doesn't hurt the untroubled spirit, either. When I say properly practiced, I mean executed in a relaxed manner, without anxiety, strain, or tension, but with confidence, inventiveness, pleasure, and ultimate pride." I wished Elizabeth Zimmermann had been my home-ec. teacher. She complimented her readers instead of making them feel stupid: "Really, all you need to become a good knitter are wool, needles, hands, and slightly below-average intelligence. Of course superior intelligence, such as yours and mine, is an advantage."

Katie and I took the leftover yarn from our sweaters and tackled the tam-o-shanters in *Knitting Without Tears*. Unlike watch caps, which fit like a sock on the head, tams are designed to drape over to the side. The pattern started at the forehead with a narrow circular band like the watch cap, but in the main part of the hat, where we doubled the number of the stitches, there was enough room to incorporate two- or three-colored designs. "Set unexpected colors next to one another," Zimmermann advised. "Get carried away." I made tiny checks with the light blue from my v-neck sweater and the denim blue from the sweater I'd made for Chuck. Katie came up with zigzags, mixing the various browns and greys from her own and Dean's sweaters. We dampened the finished hats and stretched them over her dinner plates to dry.

Katie and I were interlacing the yarns from our sweaters and our husbands' sweaters, working the multi-colored patterns like those on the Latvian mittens, but the irony of the symbolism escaped us. Katie had refused to kiss Dean more than once at their wedding reception, and we both carried our own luggage, paid for our own meals, and attended our work parties alone. At the school-house, the four of us spent most of the afternoon apart: Katie and me, Dean and Chuck.

When we all piled into a car, it was usually to visit the dairy farm a few miles away where Katie had grown up, the youngest of eight children. Her mother had died of cancer while Katie was away at college. Her father had sold the farm and its main house to one of Katie's brothers and moved into a trailer down the road. Dean and Katie often helped out on the farm and had Sunday dinners with her siblings, who lived nearby.

Dean had grown up in Green Bay, and his brothers and sisters, too, had married and settled within fifteen miles of their childhood home, so some afternoons, Katie took care of her nephews and nieces on both sides. The children played in her yard, chasing the chickens and geese Katie and Dean kept. They didn't care who they were related to by blood or by marriage, anymore than I had at their age, surrounded by my uncles and aunts on my mother's side. Although Katie asserted her independence, she and Dean were unmistakably a couple, their marriage anchored by their families. Compared to them, Chuck and I were like plants people kept in glass vials—vines that live on air, gathering nutrients through the wispy roots sunk into nothing.

Elizabeth Zimmermann, who had her own television show, wrote about accompanying her husband on his business trips and spending her afternoons knitting in hotel rooms, because she was too shy to go sight-seeing by herself. I could never admit that there was any place I couldn't go to on my own, any occasion when I wished I was closer to my in-laws, or any reason to regret that Chuck and I weren't more like other couples. What Chuck and I had in common was the pride we took in our independence, the distance we kept from everyone.

DURING THE WEEK, the two of us had dinner at home and read or watched television; I would knit all night, and he would play the guitar during the commercials. One evening in February, when it was twenty degrees below with a wind chill of minus forty, I overcooked the polenta and—distracted by a phone call—dumped it in the sink instead of the garbage can. I might as well have poured cement down the drain. The plunger and the Drano did nothing.

Under the sink, next to the Drano was a bottle of carbolic acid that was given to us when our bathtub was plugged up. Remembering how quickly the tub had started draining again, I picked up the bottle and tipped it over the sink. A lot of acid sloshed out before I could tip the bottle back. White smoke rose from the drain, and its strong sulfur smell almost choked me. When I turned on the faucet, water hissed and bubbled. Too late, I recalled my high school chemistry teacher's advice about cleaning each test tube separately to avoid mixing the chemicals in the sink and blowing up the lab.

I shut off the water and ran to the living room, where Chuck was reading. "Hey," I said. "I think I did something stupid. Maybe you should come and see."

Chuck tried to open the kitchen windows, but they were frozen shut. Smoke continued to erupt from the drain. The smell was so strong our eyes watered.

"We have to get out of here," he said, coughing. "We can leave the door open to let out the smoke. We'd better hurry."

We were both gagging, scarcely able to breathe.

I grabbed the cat, and we sprinted down the rickety stairs to the parking lot in the back of the house. We hadn't brought our coats, but I'd remembered my car key, wallet, and the blanket I'd made for the cat. My fingers were numb and my eyelashes had frozen shut. Chuck's moustache looked white. I wrapped the blanket tighter around Dorian. His deep blue eyes stared out from the beige folds.

"Let's take my car." I tossed the key to Chuck. "You drive. I'll hold Dorian."

We drove around town with the heater on high. It took my new car a good half hour to warm up.

"How long do you think it'll take the smoke to clear out?" I asked Chuck.

"I don't know. A few hours."

"Maybe we can get something to eat. I'm not planning to cook any more tonight. That polenta was really terrible."

"We can't go to a restaurant with the Buddy." Chuck called Dorian the Buddy in celebration of their friendship. "He'll bite the waiter, and we'll be asked to leave." Dorian had to be confined to the spare room when we had guests—even a temporary visitor such as the gas meter reader—because he attacked everyone who set foot in our apartment. The vet, a cat specialist and not a young man, had told Chuck's mother that Dorian was the worst cat he had ever met. To me, he only said "one of the toughest." Dorian drew blood every time.

But he was completely docile with Chuck and me. He let us hold his front paws and walk him around the apartment on his hind legs in a trick Chuck called "the Bipedal Buddy," and he was a polite passenger in any vehicle we drove. "We can't leave Dorian in the car and sit in a restaurant by ourselves," I said.

We drove to the frozen custard stand where we often got turtle sundaes—three scoops of vanilla frozen custard with hot fudge, hot caramel, pecans, whipped cream, and a maraschino cherry. The parking lot was empty, and a hand-written sign taped to the window said, "Closed Due to Bad Weather." The ink on the sign was faint, as though the pen or the writer had been on the verge of death.

"We could go to your parents' house," I said. "Maybe they'd give us food to go, but I don't want to tell them how I poured Drano and carbolic acid down the drain. It's too embarrassing."

Though it was only seven o'clock, the roads were deserted. The cold weather warning was advising people not to drive anywhere unnecessary. We passed the houses of my colleagues. "I scarcely know these people," I kept saying.

"Oh, let's just drive," Chuck said.

We circled the city several times, listening to NPR. The station played jazz that night. Chuck, I, and even the cat had written during the last pledge drive and complained, because the evening program almost always featured opera. We each promised to double our contribution if the selections could occasionally include jazz, rock, or "classical music without the human voice" as one of us so eloquently put it, but so far we had only received identical noncommittal answers. But maybe on this dangerously cold evening, the programmer was finally agreeing with us and choosing Dizzy Gillespie over Wagner. Dorian slept, woke up occasionally to scratch the blanket, and closed his eyes again. By the time we went home, three hours later, the smoke had cleared and the polenta had disintegrated. We could see our breath as we stood in the kitchen. I made Chuck promise that he would never tell anyone about our polenta odyssey. Sometimes I imagine that we are still circling the frozen city, the three of us making an itinerant family of our own, more at home in the small, dark interior of a moving car than settled inside any house.

I HAD HOPED THAT MY JOB would give me a sense of purpose or belonging, but like the rest of Green Bay, the college was old-fashioned and Catholic. The year I arrived, I was the only woman and non-Catholic on the English faculty. Other departments—philosophy, theology, history, art, biology, chemistry—had no women. Of the ten women who taught full-time college-wide, three were nuns. Most of the secular women on campus were faculty spouses, widows, or daughters who taught part-time or worked as secretaries. One of the vice presidents had hired his wife as his head secretary. My colleagues belonged to a different generation.

When I attended the dinners on campus, someone always pulled out my chair so I could sit down; later as we were heading out to a lecture or a meeting, someone else would pick up my coat and hold it for me unless I jumped up and grabbed it first. "You don't pull out chairs and hold coats for each other," I said, "so why do it for me? It makes me uncomfortable to be singled out."

At my first year-end review in his office, our division chair noticed the button-down shirt I had put on for the occasion instead of the usual orange or neon-green T-shirt emblazoned with a cartoon logo from some 10K race I'd run ("the Sampson Stomp," "the Turkey Trot," "the Armenian Martyrs' Day Race"). "You look nice," he said.

"Did you comment on the way my male colleagues were dressed for their reviews?" I asked. "If you didn't, then you should say nothing about mine."

The chair shook his head and smiled. I could only speak so frankly and ill-humoredly because he was a kind person who would never punish me for my rudeness. Still, I couldn't forgive him for his failure to use gender-neutral language.

When people from the college invited us to dinner, Chuck wore a T-shirt and jeans, and I put on a button-down shirt and grey dress pants I could have worn to church. His attire was off the charts, but mine would have been perfect had I been a man. My colleagues had chosen the same style, later called "business casual." Their spouses, in evening gowns with low backs, sat chatting about their children while I talked shop with the men. Chuck was on his own unless one of the men realized that he was the grandson of Charley Brock, the Green Bay Packer.

We were relieved when everyone had us over once and the invitations stopped. "Even my parents don't get dressed up just to eat dinner," Chuck said. We had no plans to reciprocate. Our apartment didn't have a dining room, and our living room was cluttered with Chuck's books and school supplies. Besides, I didn't want my colleagues to see me stirring a pot of soup or taking a casserole out of the oven. I had never told them that I could cook or knit.

I DIDN'T KNOW, then, that knitting only appears to be a docile activity. In one of the "knitting Madonna" paintings from the middle ages, Master Bertram of Minden portrayed Mary finishing a little crimson shirt on four needles, getting ready to cast off round the neck. Reclining at her feet, the young Jesus gazes away from his mother toward the two angels who stand on the edge of the picture; in their hands, they hold out a cross with three nails, a spear, and a crown of thorns. The crimson shirt on Mary's needles—made in the seamless method—foreshadows the seamless robe that will be stripped from him on Calgary. The painting implies that Mary is a brave mother who raises her son to die for a cause.

Even in my childhood story, knitting was the secret weapon for the princess who risked her life to save her brothers. She worked hard for seven years while they flew around helplessly. Her father failed to protect her from the evil stepmother, and her husband believed his mother's lies and threw her in jail. The only smart and resourceful fighter in her family, the princess showed no mercy to her enemies. Instead of forgiving her mother-in-law, she sent the older woman to be burned at the stake.

In the middle ages, St Sebastian was the patron saint of knitters, because the arrows of his martyrdom resembled knitting needles. Throughout history, war has inspired more women to knit than peace. A woman from Philadelphia worked as a spy during the War of Independence by hiding her messages in her balls of yarn. She sat knitting by the side of the road, and when the American army passed by, she dropped her yarn for the soldiers to pick up. The British soldiers marched past her, assuming she was a harmless farm wife. Two World Wars caused great revivals of the craft, when women all over America made socks and sweaters for soldiers. Eleanor Roosevelt attended the kick-off party for "Knit for Defense" at the Waldorf-Astoria and finished the first row of the first sweater to be sent overseas. Soon, women were knitting everywhere—in each other's homes, in parks, on buses—to contribute to the war effort.

World War II was the last war that inspired women to knit. Since then, the Armed Forces have adopted synthetic fabrics for their uniforms, and the ethos about knitting has changed. In the 1980s, around the time I started knitting, owners of yarn stores noticed that fewer women were knitting for their husbands or children; more were buying luxury yarns to make one-of-a-kind garments for themselves. Knitting was headed for another revival, this time among college-educated women. By the turn of the millennium, two women who quit their medical and legal careers to run the Yarn Company on the Upper West Side of Manhattan would be able to promote knitting among urban professionals like themselves. The book they published, *The Yarn Girls' Guide to Simple Knits*, would offer thirty patterns for women's sweaters, tank tops, hats, scarves, and ponchos. The three projects for men—given as an afterthought ("And, we have even included a few sweaters for a man in your life")—would take up just 12 of the book's 160 pages.

The Yarn Girls' Guide doesn't present knitting as a sacrifice. Each pattern is introduced with an anecdote about how easily one of the regular customers made an amazing shawl or sweater to wear to a party or a wedding reception. The cropped v-neck— "Bare That Belly"—was designed for Lisa, who wanted to show off her bellybutton ring and "washboard abs." Another customer spent the whole weekend knitting and still went out on a date on Saturday night. These women don't have to take care of boyfriends, husbands, or children. Making beautiful clothes is something they do for themselves, with other women.

If I'd lived in New York, I might have been part of this knitting revival at its beginning, but in Green Bay, the only yarn store that stocked luxury yarns went out of business the year after I moved there. At the closing-day sale, I watched dozens of women lining up with their bags of yarn and wondered where they'd come from. I had no idea that knitting was so popular, but if the store had stayed open and hosted classes and parties, these women wouldn't have shown up.

The knitters in Green Bay were wives and mothers from modest families, hard-working Catholic women unaccustomed to spending money on themselves. Many were tallying the prices on their pocket calculators while they stood in line, putting back the items they decided were too expensive, even at half price. The bags of mohair, silk, and lambswool they bought would last years. For everyday knitting—mittens, socks, and baby blankets for their children and grandchildren—they purchased polyester yarn at discount stores in the mall.

Green Bay didn't have enough Yarn Girls to replace the family knitters. The specialty yarn store was going out of business because it couldn't compete with the discount chains no matter what it stocked. The store on Milwaukee's lower east side, where I'd bought my first bag of yarn, closed soon after. By 1990, only those in Whitefish Bay, an affluent suburb of Milwaukee, and Madison, a college town, had survived. Green Bay was not so different from the world I'd left behind, where a woman married early and raised a family. The only way to have a seamless life in Japan or in a small Midwestern town was to be like everyone else—which was the one thing I couldn't do.

⌒⌒

IN MY LITERATURE CLASS, I taught a short story about a woman who loved to surround herself with beauty. The story, "A New England Nun" by Mary Wilkins Freeman, was published in 1891. Its heroine, Louisa, is a woman in her late thirties whose fiancé has finally returned from Australia to their small town to marry her. Louisa has lived happily alone during the fourteen years he was gone. Her mother and brother died and left her with a comfortable house. She can sit at her linen-covered table with her silver pitcher and pink teacup and drink afternoon tea by herself. Louisa takes such pleasure in sewing a straight seam that she sometimes rips out just to sew her stitches again. She shudders to imagine her pretty house filled with "coarse masculine belongings strewn about in endless litter." When she finds out that her fiancé is actually in love with another woman, Louisa is relieved. She tells him that her feelings have changed and she no longer wants to marry him. After he leaves, she imagines "a long reach of future days strung together like pearls in a rosary, every one like the others, and all smooth and flawless and innocent, and her heart went up in thankfulness." At the end of the story, we leave her "prayerfully numbering her days, like an uncloistered nun."

Like Louisa, Mary Freeman lost both her parents and all her siblings by the time she was thirty. She moved back from Vermont, where she'd worked as a music teacher, to her hometown of Randolph, Massachusetts, to share a house with her childhood friend Mary Wales. "A New England Nun" was published when she was thirty-nine. Ten years later, in 1901, Freeman married, but her husband became a violent and abusive alcoholic. They were separated in 1922, and at his death a year later, he left her one dollar in his will to spite her. Mary Freeman wrote no more books or essays after 1918 — when she was fifty-six — and died in 1930 of a heart attack. While living peacefully with another woman, she had predicted her marriage and given her main character a happier ending than she was to give herself. When my students thought Louisa was pathetic because she chose spinsterhood over marriage, I reminded them of the pretty cream pitcher and the crisp table cloth, the straight seam, the canary singing in the sunny window, the joy our heroine found in solitude. Even a hundred years ago, some women were happier living alone.

WHEN CHUCK AND I WENT house hunting at the end of our second year in Green Bay, we were not thinking of making a beautiful home. We were twenty-nine and thirty-two, too young, we'd assumed, to own property. With our two incomes, however, we needed a mortgage and the tax breaks that came with it.

After spending two hours with a realtor, we made an offer on a two-bedroom Cape Cod built in the 1920s with a large backyard of maple trees. We were tired of driving around, traipsing through other people's private quarters, and trying to decipher the layout diagrams on brochures. The Cape Cod was the first of five houses the realtor showed us, which we took as a sign that it was "meant to be." We bid under the asking price and told the realtor and the mortgage broker that we kept our money separate and split all the cost down the middle, that we wanted to make sure either one of us could afford the house alone in case the other died or we got divorced. When the seller refused to budge on the price or have the house professionally inspected, we didn't press. It seemed pointless to argue over a few thousand dollars when we were signing up for a thirty-year mortgage. As Chuck said, no one, not even the house inspector, could look that far into the future. "We might as well hire a psychic," he said.

The closing was in May, when my school was out. Chuck's wasn't. The following week, I transported everything I owned in the backseat of my Corolla. By Saturday, when I helped Chuck with his boxes, I was finished unpacking my own. The house had a basement office, which I set up as a writing room. Chuck could now put his desk in the spare bedroom instead of the living room. We flipped a coin for closet space and he won the walk-in closet in the master bedroom, leaving me with the smaller one in the spare room.

After our third move, Chuck and I still had not consolidated our books, music, closet space, or bank accounts. We claimed we were sparing each other—we were both notoriously unorganized—but actually, we couldn't stand anyone going through our closet, library, or checkbook. In spite of what we'd said to shock the realtor and the mortgage broker, we thought we were lucky to be with each other. No other partner would be so willing to leave us alone and let us do whatever we wanted with our time and money.

Like my seventh-grade home-ec. team, Chuck and I were united by our rebellion. While other couples negotiated over spending money, we could tell each other, "Go ahead. Live a little," every time he got another vintage guitar he didn't need or I bought state-of-the-art running shoes I would wear out in six months. When a storm hit a backyard maple, we didn't get bids from several tree trimmers like Chuck's parents advised us to do. We chose the guy with a funny ad in the Yellow Pages: "We go out on a limb for you." The guy's wife answered the phone and said her husband was "in a tree somewhere," so we hired him. "What more do we need to know?" Chuck said. "He was in a tree when we called." We didn't care how much he charged. Each of us was only paying half, and nothing in Green Bay was that expensive. We could act bold and reckless because, in reality, we were totally safe.

AFTER WORKING AS A SUBSTITUTE teacher for two years, Chuck landed a position at the only alternative grade school in town. Every child studied at his or her own pace in an open classroom, and no letter grades were ever given. His assignment was just what he'd wanted: first and second grades. He loved teaching kids who weren't yet jaded or scared about school.

Though my college was traditional, I quickly figured out my own alternative program. My motive for becoming a teacher was the opposite of Chuck's. I didn't want to change my students' lives by introducing them to exciting new ideas. I preferred self-motivated advanced-level students who scarcely needed me. Though the classes at our college were scheduled three days a week, I only met mine twice a week. The brochures from the admissions office claimed that our faculty was more committed to teaching than to academic research or artistic pursuits, but I had taken this job for its lighter teaching load. I wasn't going to give up my free time to sit in my office, serve on committees, or sponsor student organizations. "Just Say No," one of the artists told me. Eighteen years my senior, he deeply regretted he hadn't devoted himself to painting when he was my age. "Don't repeat my mistake. Do your work." His warning echoed my mother's: don't kill yourself trying to please other people, don't be like me. Of course I took it to heart.

On the days I didn't teach, I sat in my basement studio, trying to write. Since finishing graduate school, I had written several short stories set on the south side of Milwaukee, the working-class neighborhood where I had never lived. Re-reading these stories, I couldn't believe how bad they were. The characters were stuck in situations that had nothing to do with who they were. Their actions only complicated the already muddled plot. The few details I'd borrowed from real life seemed as implausible as those I'd made up.

I read again the four stories from my dissertation about a family in Japan who had lost their land after World War II. I had written the first during my second year in Milwaukee, when my grandmother Fuku's letters reminded me of my childhood visits to her house. Hiroshi hadn't allowed my grandparents to visit or write while I lived in his house. Two years after I came to the States, my grandfather, Takeo, died from a stroke. Fuku described burning incense for his spirit and bringing flowers to his grave. She was only waiting, she said, to join him. I wrote the short story, because I wanted to imagine what her life was like now that she was alone.

Even when I was a child, Fuku used to say that the purpose of our life was to endure our suffering with the help of the ancestral spirits who watched over us so we could be with them at the end. The old woman in the story lit an incense stick and contemplated her own death in the golden image of Buddha. Like Fuku, she took care of her youngest grandson while his mother worked in a factory. But her longing for beauty, her appreciation of the newly hatched cicada on her window screen, the small strawberry red patch on her quilt, the green tree frogs in the rice paddies—all that was more mine and my mother's.

Takako had sighed impatiently every time her mother made her pessimistic remarks. At the end of our summer visit, when Fuku said she might not live to see us again, Takako laughed at her and said, "Mother, you're perfectly healthy. You'll live to be a hundred years old." Later, when we were alone, Takako complained, "Your grandmother never wears that pretty maroon scarf I sent her because she thinks it's too bright for her. She's a great gardener, but she doesn't really care about beauty. I can't believe she used to write poetry before the war."

The old woman in my story was the poet Fuku might have been. I imagined her trying to celebrate her birthday alone and being moved, in spite of her grief, by the blue hydrangeas in her garden and the cicada that left its underground home to fly into the sky. It was the first story I had written about Japan. The other three stories in the dissertation featured the characters who had appeared as memories in the old woman's story—her husband who had been a former land-owner like my grandfather, her daughter who had chosen death over her unhappy marriage as my mother had done. By writing these stories, I was trying to understand something about my grandparents and my mother beyond what I knew about them as a child, but my imagination hadn't reached far enough. The characters appeared only in extreme moments of grief, joy, and understanding. The most puzzling of all was the old woman's granddaughter—a minor character so far—a fierce, all-or-nothing person utterly unlike myself. Ten years after her mother's death, she sat at a Buddhist ceremony for her mother's soul, with her back straight and her fingernails polished bright red. Surely, she wouldn't be so unforgiving. She was a girl who wanted to be a painter.

Write what you know but don't understand, my teachers had advised. I should have tried harder to understand these characters before moving on to new ones so removed from my experience. I had to go back and follow the family's story from the beginning to the end instead of skipping around to avoid the difficult parts. Why did the granddaughter want to become a painter after her mother's death? What comfort did she find in the pictures she painted? She must have wanted to forget as much as she wanted to remember. I wondered how her journey would differ from mine. She didn't go to a private school. She wouldn't be able to escape to a foreign country. My character would have to stay in the house where she'd grown up, watching her mother's perennials blooming without her year after year. What would she realize and accept that I didn't? That was the real story, the thing I was yet to understand.

Writing more stories about these characters would be like knitting the seamless sweaters I had been reworking: the same basic pattern and yet a possibility for learning something new each time. The four stories I had included in my dissertation would not be the main part of the sequence. I had so far made only the sleeves instead of the body. Now I could start over and knit my way to where the pieces connected.

~

IF I ONLY LOOKED AT THE MAPLES in the backyard and the garden Chuck and I had started, I could forget that I was living in a city with no downtown. I could write in my basement for hours. Chuck was often away, watching football or playing cards with his high school friends. The group went up to a cabin in the woods every February for their Lost Weekend, a tradition started in high school to get away from mothers and girlfriends. Chuck's old friends still didn't socialize as couples, and that was just as well.

During our first month in Green Bay, Chuck and I had stopped at one of their homes to drop off a wedding gift. The friend's wife had moved in and redecorated the apartment, covering the walls with macramé owls. On our way home in the car, Chuck said, "Wow, she's really moved in. I can't believe all that stuff she brought with her." He was making fun of the decor, so I said that maybe the couple was trying to be ironic. One of my graduate school friends had owned an old Sacred Heart painting in which the paint had cracked around Jesus' eyes, making him look like he was wearing wire-rimmed glasses. I wondered if the macramé owls were supposed to be funny in a similar way. My comment led to one of the few big fights Chuck and I ever had. As we were pulling into the parking lot behind our apartment, he called me "a fucking elitist," and I ran out of the car crying. I couldn't believe how harshly he had criticized me when he was the one who first made fun of the couple's apartment.

After a few months in Green Bay, where the lawns were decorated with plastic swans and squirrels, miniature windmills and wishing wells, I couldn't help realizing how truly stupid my remark had been. Only a fraction of the population—the kind of people who studied creative writing at graduate school—bought tacky things at rummage sales as a joke. The rest of the world collected kitsch in earnest. Chuck's friend and his wife were nothing like my graduate school friends. He worked on the railroad, and she cleaned houses. Their apartment was crammed with cheap new furniture, not the hand-me-downs Chuck and I accumulated which were our versions of the wire-rimmed Jesus (bad on purpose). I couldn't really have thought his friends were being funny. Those macramé owls scared me. I didn't want to admit that a couple who covered their walls with them were really my husband's friends.

So I held up the memory of the Sacred Heart picture like an amulet to ward off his friends, to say that *I* had nothing to do with people who collected ugly things. My comment was a rejection of Chuck as well as his friends. By making fun of the apartment, he had been trying to remind me that he had more in common with me than with people who shared his background. Ever since he was a teenager he'd felt at odds with his friends, because they were growing up to be like their parents while Chuck read *Walden* and *1984* and studied Zen. I should have laughed and said, "Come on, those owls aren't so bad," then reassured him that, of course, he was different from his friends, but they were nice people, too. But now, there was no way to explain what I'd done wrong without admitting the truth: he was right, I did look down on his friends, and even worse, so did he.

The following summer, another old friend got married and invited us to the reception at the VFW Hall. Chuck didn't introduce me to anyone while I stood by. After dinner, the men went outside for cigarettes and didn't come back until the band was starting up. Chuck hadn't smoked regularly in ten years.

"You just left me alone," I said when he finally came inside. "You could at least have introduced me."

"But everyone knows who you are. How hard is that to figure out?" he laughed. "You're a sociable person. You can speak for yourself." Then he walked away to jam with the band. He knew the musicians and had agreed to play a couple of songs including "Purple Haze" even though that didn't strike me as an appropriate wedding song.

The men at the reception were working the railroad, construction, and factory jobs Chuck had quit years ago, and the women waited tables, cleaned houses, or did light factory work. I stood on the edge of the conversation, trying to ask an occasional question so no one would think I was stuck up—an "elitist"—though that was not a word Chuck's friends would use. Since they didn't read books and we didn't watch the same TV shows or eat at the same restaurants, there was no fodder for small talk. The VFW hall was in the basement of a bowling alley—a dark, wood-paneled room with no windows. Chuck finished playing "Purple Haze" to a big round of applause and joined the guys standing around the bar. When I went out to the parking lot for air, the sun was still up. I wished Chuck and I had some mutual friends beside Dean and Katie so I wouldn't always stick out while he blended in.

I THOUGHT THINGS MIGHT CHANGE when my college started hiring new people our age. One of them was an American studies specialist whose wife had a Ph.D. in history. The couple had left Oklahoma, where she was a tenure-track assistant professor and he an adjunct, because our dean had hinted that she, too, could join the faculty as soon as there was an opening in history. In the meantime, she taught at the state university across town and was trying to revise her dissertation into a book. She and I were the same age, she was childless and athletic, and neither of us had any family close by. She had grown up in Wales, attended college in England, and gone to graduate school in Indiana. We ran into each other on campus and went out for coffee.

At a coffee shop in the downtown mall, Catherine and I discussed everything from our exercise routines, favorite books and foods, to childhood memories. I hadn't talked so much to another woman since graduate school. Katie was quiet—ten, fifteen minutes would go by without either of us saying anything while we knitted or cooked together. With Catherine, there was a new idea, story, or revelation every second. One moment, we would be debating the pros and cons of swimming for exercise, and the next, she'd be telling me about the afternoon her mother made fun of her for looking "big as a whale" in a swimsuit and her father "beat the crap out" of her with a belt for talking back to her. Catherine leaned across the table, her green eyes sparkling, her lips painted bright pink. Her dark hair contrasted with her porcelain complexion. She could never have looked "big as a whale." She was scarcely five feet tall, though no one would call her "tiny," either, since she was a body-building champion who had won trophies. In her green spandex top and tight jeans, she looked like a miniature Bionic Woman.

Catherine said she seldom wrote to her parents anymore. She had left home at eighteen, knowing she could never go back.

"I'd as soon shoot myself," she said. "But I married Tom instead." She cackled. "Don't look so shocked. Tom's okay. We get along."

I, too, had married Chuck for my visa, but I wouldn't have told anyone about it in such a flippant way. What Catherine said was unkind; still, I didn't stop to think about it. Instead, I told her something I hadn't revealed to anyone.

"The last year of graduate school when I was applying for jobs," I said, "I had nightmares every night about being back in my parents' house. I'd rather die, too, than live with them again."

"I know what you mean," she said. "You and I really understand each other."

By the time I dropped her off in front of the library, where we'd run into each other three hours earlier, I felt like I'd known her for decades.

"I had coffee with Catherine," I told Chuck when I came home. "I think we're going to be good friends. We have a lot in common."

"How do you know?" he said with a snort. "You just met her. You scarcely know each other."

Most of his football-watching friends had gone to kindergarten with him, and he had known Dean since the third grade, when they stood on the roof of their elementary school and one of them had asked the other, "Did you know that the universe has no end? What does that really mean?" I'd had a conversation like that with a girl in grade school, too, but I had no idea where she was now. For me, it was Catherine, someone else I scarcely knew, or nobody. The least Chuck could do was help me make new friends.

"Let's have her and her husband over to dinner," I suggested. "Then we can both get to know them."

"Okay," he said. "If you want."

Catherine had told me that she was a vegetarian. I was thrilled to cook for someone who ate my kind of food. I made corn-and-avocado enchiladas from *The Ananda Cook Book*, published by people who manage a meditation center out west.

At dinner, we talked about the house Tom and Catherine had rented and then about the college. Tom was several years older than the rest of us. His hair was grey and his face etched with wrinkles. He dressed like an absent-minded professor from the movies in his white button-down shirt, navy dress pants, brown penny loafers, and tan corduroy blazer with leather elbow patches. His appearance allowed him to fit in at the college, but he was as bewildered as I had been my first semester. He couldn't believe the prayers the campus chaplain said before our faculty meetings, or the comment the dean made about his wife taking his suit to the dry-cleaner's. I described how everyone had rushed to pull out my chair and hold up my coat when I was new; then I started repeating all the sexist comments I could remember my colleagues making. Chuck abruptly stood up to clear the table. I hadn't told him half the things I was regaling Tom and Catherine with.

After putting the dirty dishes in the sink, Chuck stood in the doorway between the kitchen and the dining room instead of coming in. His silence felt like a pocket of cold air, but I kept talking. When I finished the story, Catherine said, "But it's not just the college. This is the most sexist town I've ever lived in. Let me tell you what happened to Tom and me at the Y."

I suggested moving to the living room. Chuck helped me bring the coffee and the dessert and then sat down in one of the old armchairs we had inherited from his aunt. I took the other armchair so Tom and Catherine could sit together on the couch. When we were settled, Catherine resumed her story. She and Tom had joined the YMCA. When they got their membership cards in the mail, hers had Tom's last name printed on it even though she had written down her own on the application form. The membership coordinator refused to give her a new card, because she and Tom had a family membership, filed under the husband's name. "What difference does it make?" the coordinator said. "It's only a name. Aren't you happy to be married?" A week later, when they took their cat, Sandburg, to the vet, the receptionist filed the records under Tom's last name even though Catherine paid the bill with her credit card. "Even Sandburg has to have Tom's name," she said indignantly.

Tom said he'd had no idea that four hours north of Chicago, his hometown, he would find a parallel universe of pre-civil-rights prejudices. Their landlord complained that the Vietnamese immigrants were taking all the jobs in town. When a black friend of Tom's came to visit from Chicago, neighbors gawked at him. "Even Norman, Oklahoma," he concluded, "was more liberal."

"Those people are such snobs," Chuck fumed after they left. "Chicago's completely segregated, and she's from a little town in Wales. If a bunch of black people went to her hometown, I'm sure everyone would stare at them, too. They should have stayed in Oklahoma if they liked it better."

"They're new and we scarcely know them," I said, throwing Chuck's former comment back at him. "We shouldn't be so quick to judge."

He couldn't argue with that, and I was surprised by how smug I felt about defending my new friends.

TOM AND CATHERINE HAD NO IDEA that they had offended Chuck. They thought he was such a nice guy, they couldn't wait to invite us to their house. We went a few weeks later and the conversation turned once again to the faults of Green Bay. I tried to change the subject but they didn't notice. By the time we were drinking our coffee, Chuck wouldn't meet my eye. He was fidgeting with his cup, then getting up to refill it instead of asking Tom or Catherine to do it. When he came back, he turned his chair sideways and sat facing the wall. Tom and Catherine kept talking.

As we were leaving, Tom said we should go see a movie the following weekend.

"We'll think about it," Chuck said. They hugged me at the door. Chuck stepped back so they could only shake his hand.

"You don't have to go to a movie with them," I said when we got into the car.

"Believe me, I'm not," he said. "But you can go. Just tell them I'm sick." He turned on the ignition and started driving.

"No, I should tell them the truth. I'll remind them you're from Green Bay and you don't want to hear them trash it. I should have said something before we went to their house. I'm sorry I didn't."

"What good would it do to talk to them? They're such arrogant, negative people. I don't want to have anything to do with them."

Chuck himself did impersonations of the stodgy locals he encountered, like the guy who took offense when Chuck kept eating his bratwurst during the singing of the national anthem at the football stadium, or a fellow teacher who criticized the unfair trading practices of the Japanese and then turned to him with a condescending smile to whisper, "No offense" ("What do you mean?" he had shot back. "I'm not Japanese"). "Only in Green Bay," he would say at the end of these anecdotes, shaking his head. But he was mocking his hometown while Tom and Catherine—and I—were outsiders.

When Tom and Catherine made fun of Green Bay, I should have said there were a few things I liked about my adopted home. Then I could have defended Chuck and his town without calling attention to him, but I hadn't been quick or considerate enough to think of it. In fact, I was secretly thrilled by how freely Tom and Catherine criticized, how little they cared about sounding like snobs.

"I don't blame you for being upset," I said. "But Tom and Catherine will invite us again. I don't want to keep telling them that you're sick. They'll think you're a total invalid."

He didn't laugh. "Then tell them I don't want to see them because they're snobs. If you're so interested in being honest, that's what you should say."

⁓

I MADE ONE STAB AT HONESTY the following spring, when I was having dinner with Tom and Catherine at their house.

"I can't imagine being in this town without you," Catherine said in the middle of dinner. "I know we're going to be friends for life."

She and I had been meeting for coffee every week at the same cafe in the mall. I was mesmerized by the stories of her childhood. Her mother had constantly put her down—calling her fat and stupid—and her father had beaten her with a belt. She had divorced her first husband, who was English, and married Tom so she could stay as far away as possible from her parents, but now that she had her green card, she was bored with him. Once she'd turned her dissertation into a book, she might look for a job "at a real research university, not at a rinky-dink place like this." A man she'd met at an academic conference had started calling her. "He's married, too," Catherine said, "and has three small kids, so things can get a little sticky. He's beautiful, though. We were undressing each other with our eyes the whole time I was having a drink with him and his friends."

As Catherine and I walked around the shopping mall, heads turned our way, and for once, no one even noticed me. Unlike the people who stared at me, those who couldn't stop looking at Catherine were all men; they narrowed their eyes appreciatively and smiled. She smiled back, turned to me, rolled her eyes, and whispered, "Men are such pigs," in a small bright voice that was equal parts delight and disgust. I floated beside her like a peasant boy in a fairy tale with a magic cape that allowed him to disappear whenever he put it on. Safe in my invisibility, I walked, talked, even laughed. My plainness set off Catherine's beauty, but it also protected her. So long as she could tell me how bored she was, she could stay where she was with Tom instead of running off with a married man with three children.

Their dining room was decorated with the photographs Tom had taken: close-ups of her face, a shot of her in a mini-dress leaning against their car, another in a low-cut evening gown. The whole apartment was a shrine to her beauty. I couldn't picture her living anywhere else.

"I'm really glad we met, too," I said to her across the dinner table and she smiled back.

Tom piped up, "I'm sorry Chuck couldn't make it. Catherine and I really like him. Too bad he's sick so often."

I stared down at the vegetarian lasagna he had made for me. He had no idea what his wife had told me. When our eyes met but I didn't say how sorry I was, too, he frowned and the lines around his mouth deepened. I had been to their house several times by then, without Chuck. Catherine and I were thirty-two. "Friends for life" meant the next forty, fifty years. That was a long time for Chuck to be sick when he really wasn't.

"You know, Chuck's not sick," I blurted out.

They both looked up from their plates but said nothing.

"He didn't want to come because he doesn't feel so comfortable with you guys."

"What do you mean?" Tom asked.

"When we were both here back in October, we talked about Green Bay, remember? Well, Chuck grew up here. I told you before you met him the first time. Anyway, he felt kind of defensive."

"But we didn't mean anything about him. We know he's not like the rest of those people," Catherine said.

"If it bothered him, he should have said something," Tom added.

"He didn't want to make a big deal out of it," I explained. "He didn't know you guys well enough to argue with."

Catherine put down her fork and squinted at me.

"I don't think Chuck's ever going to come here," I continued, "but maybe that's okay. You're my friends. You can invite me by myself. Then I won't have to keep making excuses for him."

We finished the meal in silence before Tom and Catherine got up and went to the kitchen. They didn't come back for a long time. Finally, I left the table and went looking for them.

"We wish you hadn't told us all that stuff," Tom said. He and Catherine were standing at the counter. They hadn't loaded the dishwasher or started the coffee.

"About Chuck?" I asked foolishly.

"Yeah," Catherine said. "Now we feel weird about him."

"We had no idea he didn't like us," Tom said.

"I'm sorry," I offered. "But I didn't want to keep pretending he was sick."

Tom and Catherine never invited me to their house again. I left messages on their machine, asking Catherine to meet me so we could talk things over, but she didn't respond. After telling me all her secrets, she couldn't accept the single truth I'd revealed. Early in our acquaintance, we had stopped at my house on our way back from the cafe because she said she was eager to see the sweaters I'd made. As soon as I took a few pullovers from my dresser and held them toward her, though, she started sneezing. "I'm really allergic," she'd said, gasping and wheezing and scratching at her arms. What was harmless, even comforting, to me was poison to her, but she could have warned me. It was unfair for her to ask to see my clothes that would make her sick, or say we were friends for life so I'd feel obligated to share the truth she couldn't tolerate.

Chuck might have been relieved, then amused, to hear how she and Tom had been dumbstruck by his dislike and hidden out in the kitchen. The failure of my friendship with them could have put us back on the same side. But if I started talking about Catherine, I would start crying. Chuck would criticize and make fun of her, and I would feel angrier with him than with her. In spite of everything, I missed her. I was stunned to realize how lonely I had been.

I no longer told Chuck how hurt I was when my colleagues acted sexist and patronizing, because every time I'd come home upset during my first semester, he'd scowled and mumbled, "What did you expect?" He hadn't moved back to his hometown for my job to hear me complain. Instead of consoling me, he speculated about what I might have done to provoke the comment or gesture that upset me. So I stopped confiding in him.

Now, when other new people on the faculty invited us to dinners and parties, Chuck always gave the same excuses: he was tired, he was busy, he'd rather stay home and read. I went alone and was relieved that he hadn't come along. Practically all the new people made fun of Green Bay. Unlike the older professors who'd been raised in the Midwest, most of the new assistant professors had grown up out east. They were bitterly disappointed to be stranded in Green Bay. I couldn't say to Chuck, "You shouldn't write off all the new people. They're not like Tom and Catherine." Actually, they were worse—Tom was from a working-class Polish neighborhood on Chicago's south side and Catherine from an impoverished coal-mining town in Wales. At least they hadn't talked about their favorite restaurants in New York, the summer resorts on Cape Cod. The City, the new people said, or the Cape, as though there were no other cities or capes on the entire U. S. map. Even I cringed at their snobbishness, but I had no one else to spend time with. I said to Chuck, "You don't have to come with me. You probably wouldn't like these people. I understand."

"Good," he replied. "I never thought we had to socialize together."

"I hope you don't mind if I go. I don't have old friends like you do."

"That's up to you," he said stiffly. "I don't care who you're friends with."

Sitting alone among the new couples, I told sarcastic stories about the strangers who stared at me and practiced the few Japanese phrases they knew. People in Green Bay couldn't get over the fact that I was an English professor. "You mean you teach English to Americans? Well, I guess that's all right. You do speak pretty good," they said. Every time I heard someone say *good* instead of *well*, or *borrow* when they meant *lend* ("Can you borrow me a pen?"), I wanted to leave town and never come back. My new friends chuckled approvingly and added their own anecdotes. Driving home from their houses, I felt like a comedian on late-night TV. But when I got home, I didn't feel any more like myself.

TIRED OF WORKING AS A HOSPITAL NURSE, Katie decided to go back to school to become a counselor. She and Dean rented out the schoolhouse and moved to Albuquerque. Now, Chuck and I had no mutual friends left. Neither of us liked to plan outings, so we only went anywhere when our separate friends were in charge. Every six months or so, we resolved to "do more things" or "make some plans," only to revisit the same round of restaurants, see the few decent movies and bands that played in Green Bay, and decide it was easier to stay home.

After dinner, I got out my knitting while he chose a movie for us to watch. We sat side by side on the couch with Dorian and the knitting on my lap. One winter, we watched all the episodes of "Twin Peaks" we had recorded. When we were done, Chuck decided we should watch the PBS Civil War series. When we got to the grainy photographs of the field hospitals where soldiers were getting their legs amputated, I told him the documentary was too violent to watch after dinner.

"How could this be any worse than 'Twin Peaks'?" Chuck asked, pointing to the scene of the amputations at which he had paused the tape. "Even the people who were alive then are dead now."

"But this was real and 'Twin Peaks' was make believe," I told him.

"This picture is only in black and white."

"That makes no difference."

We laughed and argued. Our ability to argue good-naturedly, we still believed, made us special among the couples we knew. The fight about the macramé owls had been a huge exception. Most of our disagreements ended with one of us saying, "Let's talk about this later." We were able to stop so easily because we only argued about things that didn't matter: what to watch on TV, whom to vote for on the city council, which one of us should stay home to meet with the plumber. About as personal as it ever got was when one of us didn't like the other's favorite book or movie and made fun of it. We didn't consider why we were being so cruel, why we bothered to criticize so harshly. "I'm not being personal," I claimed. "I'm only being honest," he insisted. "Well, we can agree to disagree then," we concluded. Though I complained about the amputation photographs, I didn't confide in Chuck about what really frightened me: the prospect of spending the rest of my life in his hometown and failing to make something more of myself than a small-town English professor.

In the few months Catherine and I had been friends, I had told her more about my childhood memories and current worries than I had ever revealed to Chuck, but it still hadn't been an equal exchange. I offered her a few of my stories because she had confided in me first, talking about her parents' abuse without any prompting from me. After so many years away from Japan, I was no longer completely secretive about my mother's suicide or my father's remarriage but, to most people, I only gave the basic facts and quickly concluded with, "But all this was a long time ago." Catherine had emphasized her anger and bewilderment instead of downplaying them, making them loom so large that I could present my stories as small tokens in return. Still, I had never initiated a painful conversation or an exchange of confidences with her or anyone. Even with my mother it was this way. She told me she had wasted her life and I responded, was responding still. I had grown up to be exactly who I was the day she died, a person who kept everything to herself.

In the 1930s, an anonymous contributor to *The Atlantic Monthly* complained that when a woman brought out her knitting, a man felt bored and shut out. As the couple sat together, the woman silently counted her stitches instead of talking to her mate. "She is absorbed by an occupation he cannot share. She is in a sanctuary where he cannot follow." Fifty years later, as I sat next to Chuck, I was doing the same thing. My fingers repeated the same stitches over and over, knit, purl, knit, purl—an endless string of zero's.

My knitting and my writing were the only things I really cared about. Every afternoon in my basement studio, I was puzzling out the stories and beginning to understand what it was like to be my grandfather when he walked through the rice paddies his family had lost, my mother when she decided she was freeing me through her death rather than abandoning me, or even myself, had I been brave enough to stay and grieve for Takako instead of running away. The things I'd made up—the pictures my character drew of her mother's dresses, the vest she sewed from her grandmother's old *kimonos*—were intertwined with the memories I wanted to keep from my childhood. I was stitching my past into the stories for safekeeping.

But I never told Chuck what I was writing. Although I hoped to publish the stories someday, I was still struggling to understand what they meant to me. I couldn't sit at my desk and scrutinize my past, both the beauty and the pain, unless my everyday life was like a period of rest after a hard run. I couldn't live with someone who asked about my writing and demanded to share my thoughts.

Like the spy knitting in plain sight, I was hiding my secrets in my balls of yarn. Knitting was a pantomime of writing. In both, I longed to make a seamless whole—to combine fact and fiction, imagination and memory, color and texture, beauty and form, repetition and invention. But in the rest of my life, I only knew how to keep things separate: my job, my writing, my marriage, my past, my present, all like pieces of cloth cut up beyond repair. Chuck gave me the steady everyday life that counter-balanced my writing, but he could only do that by not knowing the truth. I was turning him into what he said his parents were: boring and harmless, a person who left me alone. How could he forgive me if he knew?

He restarted the tape, setting in motion more pictures from the war that had nothing to do with my past. "Have it your way," I said with an exaggerated sigh, pretending to give in. My fingers slid back and forth over the yarn, and the stitches kept multiplying.

Shawls

I N THE NINETEENTH CENTURY in Europe, wearing a shawl gracefully was considered a mark of good breeding. Even rich women lived in poorly insulated houses, and the Empire-style dresses of the period were thin and low cut. In England, knitting lace shawls became a popular hobby among the leisured ladies who sat all day in their drawing rooms.

Lace is produced by deliberately creating holes in the fabric, by knitting two stitches together and looping the yarn over the needle to make another stitch. The holes are repeated at regular intervals to form scallop shells, frost flowers, trellises, peacock feathers, maple leaves, waterfalls, and so on. Lace requires very fine yarn, and the yarn-over stitch is not firmly anchored in the stitch in the previous row, so it's easy to snag and tear. Only well-to-do women could wear lace shawls or knit them as a hobby.

Young English ladies were taught to hold their right-hand needle daintily and unsteadily like a pen instead of grasping it firmly under the palm. Lace-knitting was supposed to show off their pretty hands and downcast eyes to any suitor sitting nearby. Like the flower arrangement and tea ceremony lessons my friends took in Japan in the 1970s, knitting prepared a woman for marriage. Downcast eyes were popular in our century, too. An article I read in a teen magazine said we should look at a boy's throat while he was talking to us so he would be smitten by our modest downcast eyes. This advice was accompanied by instructions—complete with a diagram—on how to put on mascara, eyeliner, and eye shadow.

If I had to look at a boy's throat instead of his face, how would I know when he was finished speaking? Even if his voice had trailed off, maybe he was only pausing to collect his thoughts. Without eye contact, a face-to-face conversation was no better than a phone call. I wondered how anyone could read advice like this and not feel hopeless. I gave up on the makeup because I couldn't close my eyes and still see where the eye shadow should go. Short of making a life-size copy of the diagram and holding it up to my face like a stencil, the whole maneuver was physically impossible.

Since I attended an all-girls school, there were only two boys my age I ever talked to—brothers who used to live next door to my family until the younger of them, Tadashi, and I were ten. Our mothers had stayed friends beyond the move, and because their father, Mr. Kuzuha, worked with mine, they were among the few old friends I was allowed to see after my mother's death. When I visited their house, their mother cried and reminisced about Takako. I listened to music, watched TV, and played cards or board games with Tadashi and Makoto, who had grown up seeing my mother every day. At their house, I could mention her any time I felt like it. "Remember that hike we went on when it got really foggy? My mother was sure she knew the way but we were actually walking around in circles?" I could ask, and the boys would nod. "When the fog cleared, we were standing almost exactly where we'd started out and she was the first to laugh about it." "Yeah," one of them might answer. "We sure got lost a lot when we went anywhere with your mom."

Tadashi had spent two weeks at my grandparents' house one summer with my mother, brother, and me. Wherever we were, he was my ally growing up. Makoto, three years older, tried to boss us around, but I sympathized with him, too, for being the older of two children. Between the brothers, I was an honorary middle child, a peacemaker instead of the outcast I had become at home. After Takako's death, Tadashi and Makoto were more like my brothers than Jumpei, who followed Michiko around as though she were his real mother. I couldn't imagine not looking them in the eye as we talked. If I stared at their throats instead, they would think I'd lost my mind.

Michiko must have known how important the brothers were to me. When I was sixteen, she told my father that their mother had discovered me writing love letters to Makoto's roommate at college—a boy I'd only met once at their house and whose face I could not even remember. Hiroshi believed her lie and never asked me about the supposed letters. He just said I was no longer allowed to see the family.

To prevent me from ignoring his order and going to their house anyway, Michiko told me that Tadashi's mother had complained I was no longer the nice girl I used to be. I didn't yet know what a big liar Michiko was, so I thought I had made some careless remark that offended my mother's friend. I didn't find out the truth until Tadashi and I were nearly forty. By then, we had been out of touch for decades, and we lived so far apart. All we could do was exchange occasional holiday cards. After Michiko had lied to me, Tadashi's mother had continued to invite me to their house, but I thought she was a hypocrite to sound so pleasant on the phone while talking behind my back. I declined the invitations with the lamest excuses till she stopped calling. Michiko was able to keep me from people who loved me, because I assumed the worst about everyone, including myself.

THE NINETEENTH-CENTURY FEMINIST and dress reformer Abba Woolson wanted to abolish lace shawls from women's wardrobes. She believed they hindered movement, encouraged false modesty (they made women "hide and confuse the contours of this common human form, as if they were a disgrace"), and cut off circulation. She wished every woman would put on a "simple, sleeved garment" and go to work instead of sitting all day with their useless needlework.

By the time I became a knitter, lace was no longer quaint, fussy, or modest unless it was on a doily. A few years after my falling-out with Catherine, a store called Leather and Lace opened in the downtown mall where we used to have coffee. The mannequins in the window were dressed in lacy camisoles and leather pants, shiny spandex leotards and poofy little-girl skirts with lace trims. Catherine would have loved those clothes. They were perfect for the trashy Lolita look she cultivated. She had been so thrilled and offended when men stared at her. I remembered the quick smile she flashed at them before turning away in scorn. Flirtation was all about keeping men guessing, about hovering between availability and aloofness, and lace was her favorite fabric because her skin peeked tantalizingly through the holes. Catherine had left Tom and was living in San Antonio with a karate instructor. I heard she was studying to be a New Age healer with crystals and herbs. I pictured her practicing yoga in the white lace leggings she used to wear with her weightlifting outfit. I shouldn't have been surprised when she offered me a life-long friendship and then refused to speak to me. She had always been a mistress of mixed messages.

My friendship with her was the opposite of my marriage. From the start, Chuck never confused me with grand promises and mixed messages. He didn't make declarations of forever. Like the boys from my childhood, Chuck was my everyday ally and friend. I hadn't been attracted to Tadashi and Makoto because I knew them too well. But Chuck had put himself through school by driving a cab, working on the railroad and in factories, and playing bass at weddings; he'd lived in a one-room schoolhouse with a bunch of guys and their dogs, all of them hiking to the bluff over Lake Michigan in the middle of the night to howl at the moon. When we first met and started running together, I was thrilled to hear his stories, but I thought it would be all right if he never asked me out as long as I could always know him in some way—like a brother who lived far away but stayed in touch. I didn't experience the desperate, all-or-nothing love my mother must have once felt for my father. I thought I was lucky to meet someone I could love and admire in a logical, sensible way.

My friendship with Catherine was as tempestuous as a love affair gone wrong. We got to know each other quickly and became inseparable; she promised to be with me forever, only to ignore my phone calls. I wouldn't have been drawn to her if I really believed that love was logical or sensible, but I didn't know that yet.

THREE SUMMERS AFTER CHUCK and I bought our house, his grandfather, Charley, died unexpectedly from a brain aneurysm. He was in the hospital for just two nights, never regaining consciousness. Left to live alone for the first time in fifty years, Chuck's grandmother, Alice, moved to a small apartment where it was easier to manage on her own. Though she was careful not to complain, her pale blue eyes had a fragile, surprised look.

As Christmas approached, I wanted to knit her a present, but I was stumped about what to make. Alice didn't wear sweaters. She put on dress pants and blouses for formal occasions and jeans and sweatshirts for the casual. She had no use for hats and mittens since she didn't go outside much in the winter. After reviewing the numerous knitting books I had collected, I chose the huge, round shawl from Elizabeth Zimmermann's *Knitter's Almanac*. It was by far the most beautiful garment I could possibly make. There was nothing weak or languishing about this shawl. It had heroic proportions, like a magic cape. It measured seventy inches across, and the yarn-over holes lined up to form a twelve-petaled flower. The light blue yarn, flecked with silver, was the color of Lake Michigan on a winter morning. Alice wore the shawl as she sat in her new living room, and she kept it draped over the back of her chair.

But she didn't stay in that apartment very long. By Christmas of the following year, she was diagnosed with cancer. When the chemotherapy didn't shrink her tumors, she moved first to an assisted-living apartment and then to a nursing home. I visited her every week, while Chuck stayed home. He said it was too depressing to go there, to see her "in that hospital room with a metal cot."

Growing up, he had been close to his grandparents. When he was four, his family was living in Milwaukee, where Dick was finishing college, and Chuck already had two younger sisters. Every weekend, he traveled to Green Bay by himself to spend time with Alice and Charley. His mother put him on the train at one end, and Alice picked him up at the other, accompanied by Chuck's teenage aunts. "My grandparents were more like my parents when I was young," he'd said, "because Dick and Mary were busy with my sisters."

It was hard for Chuck to see Alice in a nursing home, because he had known her as a young woman—a mother of teenagers—while to me she was always old. I should have advised him to visit her anyway. She needed him now, just as he had needed her back then, but I seldom told people what to do unless they were my students. When friends asked for advice, I simply described what I knew they wanted to do, making it sound like I had thought of it. Chuck, who hated giving or accepting advice, didn't ask me what to do. Nor did he expect me to lie for him, but I exaggerated how busy he was to spare Alice's feelings. In the summer, he really was out of town often, camping in one wilderness area or another.

"Don't you get lonely?" she asked me once.

"Oh, no," I laughed. "I love having the house to myself."

"I wish I'd been more independent," she said. "All my adult life, I was a football wife."

If she hadn't gotten sick, I could have said, "But you're on your own now." Sitting in the nursing home with the heart and teddy bear decals pasted on the windows, a thin curtain separating Alice's side from her roommate's, I couldn't even think of the right platitude to say. Alice politely changed the subject. Seven years had passed since that first awkward dinner at our apartment. I took her shopping and drove her to doctors' appointments. Alice and I still turned to small talk, though, when the conversation got too personal. It was the way we'd both been raised.

Alice's family had left Sweden before she was old enough to attend school. Her younger brother, Arnold, had been a baby so he remembered nothing, and their parents didn't talk about the old country once they settled in Nebraska though they spoke Swedish at home. One Christmas, Arnold was in the Nativity pageant at their Lutheran Church. He marched onto the stage with a paper crown on his head and said, "Greetings. We are the three wise guys of the Orient." Their parents didn't understand why everyone laughed. "They were typical immigrants," Alice said, "very anxious to fit in. They wanted to be American, but they didn't understand English." Alice wanted to go back to Sweden to see her childhood home and look up her relatives, but she never got a chance. I wondered if I, too, would someday remember the places of my childhood in the same scattered way she did: a stand of trees on a playground, the layout of a particular house, a favorite cousin — if I would cling to the memory no one could share.

When Alice died, Chuck was camping in Northern Michigan. I couldn't recall what day he said he was coming back or if he'd told me. His plans depended on the weather and the condition of the campground. He didn't always come home when he said he would.

I drove to the local camping equipment store and found the telephone number of the ranger station nearest the campsite, but the ranger wasn't there. All I could do was leave a message on the answering machine. Chuck came home two days later, just in time for the funeral. He said he had been standing near his campsite in the late afternoon when the ranger walked up to him and asked, "Are you Chuck Brock? You're wanted at home. Your grandmother passed away."

The funeral was at the Congregational church Alice had attended with Charley. The pastor talked about the afternoon, two weeks prior, when he'd visited Alice at the nursing home. Her condition was quickly worsening then, but she could still hear us and respond. "Her two granddaughters were talking to her," the pastor said. He meant Chuck's sister Chris and me. I cried as we stood up to sing—"This is my Father's world, and to my listening ears/ All nature sings, and round me rings the music of the spheres"—a hymn I had learned in the seventh grade, because it had been the favorite of our school's founder, the American missionary woman. Alice was leaving us just when I was becoming her family.

Chuck didn't cry at the funeral, but he grieved in his hard, solitary way. Nearly three years later, he said, out of the blue as we were driving somewhere, "When I was feeling so bad because my grandmother died. . . ." I don't remember the rest of that sentence, just that the point he was making had nothing to do with her. He could only mention his grief to me by slipping it into an incidental remark after enough time had passed. I knew I was supposed to look up, nod, and say nothing more.

Chuck never told me why he'd gone to a wilderness campsite when his grandmother was dying, leaving a few days after she had stopped responding to anyone's voice (He said, "She could be like this for months.") or if he regretted making that trip. My grandmother was living alone in Japan, surrounded by the land she and my grandfather had lost. She had stopped writing to me a few years after I moved to Green Bay, because she could no longer see well enough. Long before that, I could tell she was having a hard time holding her pen—her handwriting had gotten fainter with each letter, as if her words were beginning to evaporate. How could I advise Chuck to stay and see his grandmother through her final days when my whole life was like a wilderness camp I'd gone off on to get away from my family?

I fooled myself into thinking I was respecting his privacy, but the truth was, I didn't want to hear. My mother had confided the worst of her unhappiness to me, and it had done us no good. I was relieved that Chuck kept quiet until he had gotten accustomed enough to his feelings to mention them in passing. I didn't believe grief ever went away. It could only be contained.

After Alice's death, my father-in-law meant to save the shawl I had made for her, but someone had already taken her clothes to Goodwill. I knitted myself another in purple to remember her by. The yarn, from Shetland, was very thin and tightly twisted. Shetland is a group of about 100 islands, fewer than 20 of them inhabited. Even the inhabited islands are more isolated than the wilderness campsite where Chuck had gone to hide from his grandmother's death. As long as he stayed away, he must have been thinking, nothing would happen to her.

130 ocean miles separate Shetland from the northern coast of Scotland. In the late nineteenth century, lace shawls knitted in Shetland were sold all over Europe. The infants' christening shawls, made by the best knitters, could slide through a wedding ring. My shawl started at the center with nine stitches and became larger and larger as it went around the circle, increasing the number of stitches at regular intervals until there were five hundred and seventy-six stitches squeezed around the needle. I was knitting in circles, my path expanding from the center out.

Traditional lace was made in Italy in the fifteenth century by cutting tiny holes in linen and pulling out the thread. In knitting, the holes are constructed with yarn-over stitches. You add a hole instead of tearing it out. It would be years before I understood what the difference meant. You can build what is usually taken away. Loss can expand as well as constrict us: an absence is also an opening.

THREE

Fair Isle

IN THE FIRST HALF of the nineteenth century before lace-knitting became a popular cottage industry, the farm women of Shetland made mittens, socks, and caps to sell to the sailors on their merchant ships. Their favorite patterns were yellow, white, green, or blue zigzags, checkers, x's and o's, and diamonds on a variegated background of black, red, and brown. The knitters worked with two or more skeins of yarn, holding the accent colors in one hand and the background color in the other. The colors not being worked were carried in the back and loosely twisted with the one being knitted. This interlacing method is still called "Fair Isle knitting" after one of the islands. When the novelist Sir Walter Scott visited the Fair Isle in 1814 with a party of Commissioners for the Northern Light-House Services, he bought mittens and caps to send home. He warned his wife in a letter that they should be "well scoured, for of all the dirt I ever saw, that of the Fair Isle is transcendent."

The women of the Fair Isle must have been too busy knitting, cooking, growing vegetables, herding sheep, and taking care of their families, to keep their houses tidy. They were the opposite of my stepmother, who did nothing but clean. Michiko didn't bake, sew, knit, embroider, garden, entertain her neighbors, or read. She threw out the tapestries Takako had made, saying they were cluttering the house.

My mother hadn't had time to sweep and vacuum every day. Between when I was six and ten, when our family lived in a large apartment complex near the sea, I often came home from school to find a dozen women from our building seated around our dining table with their embroidery. Getting together with the neighbors was one of the few things a married woman could to do for entertainment. Everyone was talking and laughing. Some came just to drink tea, eat the cookies my mother had baked, and admire the flowers in the garden—the zinnias and the snapdragons Takako would cut for them, the pink "Queen Elizabeth" roses she sketched and photographed, the peonies and the hydrangeas she'd transplanted from her parents' house. My mother might have been the only one who really loved embroidery. "Your mother made such beautiful things," her friends said at her funeral. "But it was her company we came for."

Twenty years later, I found the folk-art borders Takako used to stitch on her tapestries—stars, flowers, birds, and dancers holding hands—in my books about Latvian and Hungarian knitting. As Fair Isle knitting spread from Shetland to Scandinavia and Eastern Europe, women copied their embroidery and cross-stitch patterns on to their mittens and sweaters. The stars, flowers, birds, and dancers traveled from country to country, now in cross-stitch, now in knitting. The wedding mittens of Latvia were made in the Fair Isle method, using some of the same geometrical motifs. Knitters in Norway became famous for their *luskofte*, or lice-patterned sweaters, made in dark wool with a sequence of patterned bands. They only used white in places, like the hem, where it never showed. Between the bands of roses, stars, or stags, the Norwegian knitters put in tiny dots called "lice stitches" (after the insect) to decorate every inch of the garment. None of these women saw embellishment as clutter. Even lice could inspire a lively pattern.

~

TAKAKO HAD BEEN HAPPY at the apartment surrounded by her friends, but after we moved to a single house up on a hill, she was alone every afternoon. The women in our new neighborhood had retired husbands who were home all day expecting to be waited on. Takako's old friends couldn't easily travel the few miles that separated them. None of them could drive; besides, married women didn't leave their neighborhood except to go grocery-shopping or to visit their children's schools.

By my fifth year in Green Bay, I, too, was stuck in the house with no one to talk to. I dreaded going outside except to run. Strangers in grocery stores and shopping malls continued to ask me about Japan, and our neighbors stared as I worked in the garden. I had stopped socializing with the new couples at my college because their bitterness depressed me. Chuck was the only person I felt comfortable with, but we had less and less to talk about.

The two of us had a good time when we visited Dean and Katie in New Mexico or went sightseeing in the cities where I attended academic conferences or gave readings. If I found another job in a real city, he said, he would quit his and come along. But looking through the national job list every October left me too exhausted to apply to any. Since my big move from Kobe to the U.S., I'd only migrated two hundred miles north—from Rockford to Milwaukee to Green Bay. Chuck had traveled the same distance and ended up where he'd started. Now, the two of us could hardly manage an evening out.

Whenever he told me he was willing to move, Chuck said in the same breath, "But it's okay if we stay here, too." He complained that Green Bay was a horrible place, only to add that most cities in the U. S. were worse. He mentioned wanting to move to Canada or Mexico or even Europe, then suggested finding a bigger house in our neighborhood or building a summer cottage in a nearby town. He must have been as confused as I was. If we could have talked about how terrified we both were to stay or to leave, we could have helped each other move on or accept the home we'd made. But discussing the future felt as overwhelming as planning an expedition to the Arctic. Every time I geared up for a talk, Chuck acted tired and put out, so I told myself that we were comfortable enough where we were.

In the end, I decided to try harder to settle into Green Bay without bothering Chuck about it. If I made friends away from the college and stayed busy, everything might still fall into place. I was trying to transform the grey stretch of my routine into colorful Fair Isle knitting. Like my mother, I turned to needlework and other women to decorate the empty space.

AT THE ANNUAL ART FAIR held in the parking lot of the downtown mall, I found three women sitting on folding chairs and making yarn on old-fashioned spinning wheels. One was using fleece that had been cleaned and processed to the consistency of cotton candy. The second had clumps of greasy wool with pieces of hay stuck in it. The third held a white rabbit on her lap; wisps of long hair came off its belly and turned into yarn. The women looked like three fairy godmothers in a folk tale, each offering a gift. The one with the clean, cotton-candy wool was a psychology professor at my college.

A plump woman in her late thirties with short dark hair, Sharyl was wearing jeans, a white T-shirt, and a hand-woven vest.

She and her husband, Bob, had moved to Green Bay from Colorado. They lived out in the country and had no children. Sharyl knew how to spin and weave but not to knit, so we decided to exchange lessons. Her large ranch house had a "fiber room" with two looms, three spinning wheels, and skeins of yarn hanging from the ceiling. Bob, who taught computer science at the technical college across town, had taken spinning and weaving classes with Sharyl. "We needed something to do during the long winters here," he said. He went back to the rug he was making and didn't talk again the whole afternoon. Even their Shetland sheepdog, debarked by his former owner, was quiet.

For our lessons, Sharyl had copied articles about spinning history, equipment, and techniques. On our first day, she had me practice handling the wool by itself—stretching it out, pinching and twisting it between my thumb and finger. The second time, I learned how to treadle the empty wheel. During our third lesson, Sharyl finally asked me to sit down at the wheel with the wool. The wheel, which had spun smoothly enough when it was empty, wobbled and stopped and spun backward while I clutched at the wool. My yarn broke and tangled.

Aside from scribbling a few basic instructions on a crumpled piece of paper, I hadn't prepared a lesson. I thought Sharyl could watch me and learn by trial and error. In spite of my lame teaching, the scarf she had started looked like a scarf while the matted and tangled fiber on my bobbin resembled mutant maggots. Every time she made a mistake, though, Sharyl muttered, "I'm never going to learn how to do this." "Don't worry," I said. "You'll get the knack of it eventually." She quit when the scarf was several inches long and slightly crooked. When I told her that it would look straight enough wrapped around her neck, she shook her head and said, "I'm never going to be that good at this. It's too frustrating."

Sharyl had no patience for being a beginner, because she was already so good at everything. She had made straight A's in school, finished her Ph. D. at twenty-seven, and gotten tenured a few months before her thirtieth birthday. Maybe I was lucky to have received D's and F's in several subjects and failed my driving test four times. My mediocre performance at the spinning wheel didn't surprise me any more than my inability to parallel park. I bought my own wheel and started practicing by myself.

THE SPINNING WHEEL TURNS WOOL into yarn simply by twisting it. All a spinner has to do—theoretically—is hold the prepared wool with both hands, treadle the wheel with one foot and slowly stretch the fiber so it gets twisted evenly, and let go of the resulting yarn to wind on to the bobbin. If you allow too much twist before letting go, though, the yarn tangles on itself; too little, it breaks. A skilled spinner can adjust her treadling speed and the tension of her hands to the consistency of the fiber and produce perfectly smooth, soft yarn. But since finished yarn is usually plied (two or three strands twisted together, also on the wheel, for strength), the thick and the thin spots will combine to make a fairly uniform yarn even if each strand is bumpy and uneven, so long as it doesn't tangle or break. The irregularity adds to the homey texture of the homespun.

After a month of practice, I came up with enough yarn from the plain fleece Sharyl had given me, to knit a watch cap. Sharyl and Bob took me to a spinning festival near Madison, where I bought a bag of "rainbow-dyed fleece," which looked like psychedelic cotton candy with streaks of green, blue, purple, pink, and red. I spun a handful of each color, and from the dozen walnut-sized balls I got, I knitted a pair of socks with Fair Isle checkers.

FARM WOMEN OF SHETLAND, too, had used whatever colors they could get for the brightest, most striking combination. The sheep on the islands were famous for the variety of their natural colors—white, cream, light brown, dark brown, reddish brown, grey, black—and lichens, berries, nuts, onion skin, indigo, and other plant materials could produce greens, yellows, blues, and reds. The caps the women sold to sailors were colorful enough to be spotted from a long way off. It was only in the twentieth century that "natural" came to imply subdued earth tones, because, compared to the artificial dyes that produced the lime green and the sky blue of my rainbow-dyed socks, the lichens and the indigo were quite subtle.

Although the spinning wheel was not invented till the middle ages, spinning itself was practiced as far back as 15,000 B. C. The early spinners used the spindle—a long stick with a round top to twirl by hand—or just rolled the fiber a little at a time against a convenient smooth surface like their thigh. Sheep's wool was available in Mesopotamia as early as 4,000 B. C. Cotton was cultivated in India around 3,000 B. C. The Salish Indians kept small white dogs—now extinct—exclusively for their hair. A woman at the spinning fair was selling watch caps knitted from her Samoyeds' hair. The caps had the unmistakable odor of dog. I wouldn't have wanted to wear them in rain or fog, but they would have been perfect for running in the country where farm dogs chased me. The meanest German shepherd would have tucked tail and fled, if he could have been persuaded that I was a one-hundred-and-and-twenty-pound Samoyed.

The Chinese had a monopoly on silk for centuries starting around 2,500 BC. They exported caravans of finished silk textiles through the Silk Road but refused to reveal the source or methods of its production. Finally, in the sixth century, two Persian monks who used to live in China returned there and smuggled silkworms back to Constantinople in the hollows of their bamboo canes. All the silk produced in the Middle East and Europe until the nineteenth century could be traced back to these stolen worms. Spinning could transform dog hair into hats, moth cocoons into scarves, and religious men into industrial spies. I hoped it would change me, too, into someone who could live happily in a remote town.

AT THE MONTHLY GATHERINGS of the local spinning group I joined, I met several women who kept angora rabbits. Unlike sheep's wool, rabbit hair didn't have to be washed, degreased, or fluffed up in preparation. It could even be spun right off the animal on one's lap. The rabbits were bred for their docile temperament as well as for the quality of their hair. The women who had them lived in town, not on a farm, and bought them treats—organic greens, blueberries, papaya—at the few high-end grocery stores that were still novelties in our area in the early 1990s. When the rabbits got sick, they were rushed to the veterinary hospital where Dorian had terrorized his cat doctor, to see the exotic animal specialist.

The farmers who sold wool at the spinning festival had also offered lamb skins—tiny white fur puddles with four legs sticking out—and ice chests full of lamb chops packed in cellophane. The sheep whose fleece I bought had been allowed to live past their first edible phase, but when they got too old to produce good wool, they, too, would be sent to the slaughter house. No one ate angora bunnies even on a farm. Unlike silk, which was produced by plunging the unhatched cocoons into boiling water, angora was a luxury fiber harvested from pampered pets. As a vegetarian, I told

Chuck, I had no excuse not to raise my own cruelty-free fiber. He agreed.

The first angora I got, from a woman in my spinning group, had black tresses cascading down her forehead like the beauties painted by Dante Gabriel Rossetti. The hair on Rossetti's back and belly was silver. The second rabbit, from an award-winning breeder near the Minnesota border, was pure white. I named her Frida, after Frida Kahlo's self-portrait in the enormous white collar. To clip their hair, first I tried the electric shears from a farm equipment store. The roaring, grinding noise didn't upset the rabbits, who just sat there. I switched to plain scissors because the noise scared me.

Since the rabbits grew back their hair every eight weeks, I soon had several shoe boxes of clipped hair. I spun some of it on its own but sent the rest to a professional mill to be mixed with sheep's wool. The blend was easier to spin—sheep's wool, once prepared, is less slippery than angora—and more versatile. Alone, angora was too warm, soft, and feminine for most projects. With the hand-spun yarn of 60 % Rossetti and 40 % Anonymous Romney Sheep from Ohio, I knitted the grey socks Chuck wore to watch the Packer games in the winter. In the crowded stadium of 50,000 spectators, I'm sure he was the only person wearing rabbit socks (or eating his bratwurst during the singing of the national anthem).

For myself, with 100 % Rossetti, I designed a scarf in the shape of a fox. The main part of its body was a tube long enough to wrap around my neck; the gradual decreases I'd learned from my hats and socks helped shape the head to taper toward the pointed nose. To finish, I picked up a few stitches each to knit the tail, feet, and ears and sewed on buttons for the eyes and the nose. The nose button and the button loop hidden under the tail allowed the fox to stay curled around my neck; the silver bugle beads I sewed on the feet made the clicking sound of claws. The Rossetti fox was the first thing I'd figured out how to make entirely on my own. If I didn't already have a job, Chuck said, I could make more to sell at fiber festivals around the country. They could be advertised as "Cruelty-free Fur" (my idea) or "Vegetarian Fox" (his). My booth at the fair would have an ice chest full of marinated tofu and meatless meatballs. There would be a big picture of Frida, Rossetti, and Dorian—my version of a peaceable kingdom.

Frida and Rossetti lived in cages in my basement writing studio, but they hopped around our house for a few hours every night while I watched to make sure they weren't chewing the furniture or electrical cords. Dorian jumped up on the couch and didn't come down until the rabbits were safely back in their cages. Frida and Rossetti looked more like dust mops with feet than like the artists they were named after. As they made their way across the room, their heads bobbed back and forth, causing their long tufted ears to sway. Chuck at first believed Dorian was eyeing the rabbits from the couch, waiting to attack like a deer hunter in his tree stand. He said it was unwise to have prey and predator loose in the same small space. But one afternoon, Dorian was eating his food when I brought the rabbits upstairs. He took one look at them, spat out the food, and fled to his perch.

"Come on, Buddy," Chuck said. "You're pathetic. You're supposed to eat them. Don't you know about the food chain?"

Actually, Chuck was afraid of the rabbits, too. He agreed to feed Frida and Rossetti in my absence but not to take them out of their cages, because they might bite him.

Frida and Rossetti never bit anything except their food; they practically went to sleep on their backs while I was clipping hair off their chests. But Chuck was serious. He had gotten bad rabbit karma in high school from the Easter bunny his mother had bought for his younger brother, Brian. In the middle of the night before Easter, the rabbit, which was left in a carrying cage outside Chuck's room in the basement, started grunting and thumping loud enough to wake him up. Chuck figured that the rabbit was unhappy about being stuck in the little cage, so he let him out and went back to sleep. In the morning, Brian came downstairs and found the rabbit dead in the pile of saw dust from their father's carpentry project. He cried, their mother got upset, and everyone concluded—for some reason—that the rabbit had died from eating saw dust.

"Maybe it wasn't your fault," I suggested. "I bet the rabbit was so restless because he was sick. He could have died even if you hadn't let him out. A healthy rabbit isn't going to eat saw dust and die."

Chuck had never thought of that, but he didn't seem comforted in the least. "That's possible," he shrugged. "But Mary was sure I'd killed him."

Chuck had a lot of stories about his mother getting upset with him, though he usually tried to tell them as a joke. She locked him out of the house when he was five, because he'd thrown earthworms at her in the garden. A few years later, Chuck and his two sisters barricaded themselves in the bathroom while Mary was yelling at them. One by one, they crawled out of the window and went to play with their friends. "I don't know how long Mary was pounding on that door, thinking we were still in there," they said, laughing. Chuck and his siblings called their parents by their first names. Telling funny stories about Dick and Mary was one of the few things they had in common.

Chuck's sister Chris had married right out of high school as their parents had. Her three sons were always wrestling in the kitchen, riding their tricycles down the hallway, playing catch in the dining room. Chris or her husband would yell, "Stop that. I'm going to count to ten." But when the time was up, no one was sent to their room. Chuck teased, "Watch out. Russ and Chris are still counting," which made the boys act more obnoxious.

One Thanksgiving, Chuck had a big argument with Chris and Russ, who insisted that all welfare recipients were deadbeats. In the car going home, Chuck rolled his eyes and said, "Chris was driving me nuts with that snide tone of hers. I had a flashback about shoving her face in a snow bank, so I had to stop." Another afternoon, Brian and his wife, Dawn, had the whole family over for one of their three sons' birthday. Dawn belonged to the conservative Lutheran synod that didn't celebrate Halloween because it was a witches' holiday. She didn't let their children go trick-or-treating, and she insisted that "Barney" was the only wholesome show on TV. When Chuck and I started singing off key in our bad Barney imitation, Dawn walked out of the dining room where we were having cake and went upstairs. Brian shook his head at us and said, "You guys." Even their sister Carrie who wasn't at all religious, said, "I don't know. I think Dawn's really mad." When Dawn came back downstairs, we apologized, and nothing more was said about our bad behavior.

"My family," Chuck said on our way home. "At least they leave us alone. They don't expect us to see them much just because we live fifteen minutes away."

Chuck's family didn't pressure us about anything. "Oh Chuck," they usually laughed when he tried to shock them with his ultra-liberal opinions. "You always had your own ideas about things." To be dismissed so casually must have given him a lonely, excluded feeling; he was forever the oldest child sent to his grandparents' house so his parents could care for the younger children. Chuck picked fights with his family to get their attention, to make them notice how different he was forced to be from them, but if any of them felt bad, they didn't show it.

As we drove away, Chuck and I made fun of the things his parents and siblings had said and laughed about the visit. His family was misguided but they meant well, we said to each other. Unlike Hiroshi and Michiko, Chuck's parents loved him even though they hadn't known, for decades, how to talk to him. In spite of their disagreements, his sisters and brother looked up to him as the oldest. In all the stories they told about their childhood, Chuck was the ring-leader, the hero of their escapades. He couldn't just write off his family the way I did, but I never stopped to consider how much more complicated and painful his situation was than mine. So long as Chuck remained an outsider to his family, I could pretend that I belonged to them, too. I could claim them as much as he did, and no more.

IF WE WERE TO RECONSTRUCT the missing arms of Venus de Milo, she might be holding a spindle in her right hand and a distaff (the stick around which the flax was wound) in her left. The positions of her shoulders suggest that her right arm was extended and her left arm bent. Venus, the goddess of love, brought a man and a woman together to produce the thread of new life. She could easily have been portrayed as a spinner.

If I had really wanted to become a part of Chuck's family or the community we lived in, I should have had children. Then I would have been one of the colors in a Fair Isle sweater, intertwined with those around me to help the design continue and repeat itself. Often, it's the one color that almost clashes—specks of ochre in an otherwise green and blue composition—that completes the harmony and enlivens the pattern. I could have been that color for Chuck's family, but I didn't like children even when I was a child. In the summers at our grandparents' house, I walked in the woods by myself while my brother played in the yard with our younger cousins. I snuck out during afternoon naps to swim in the river alone, to get away from the crying babies and my aunts fussing over them. As I dove into the water, I wondered how terrible the grownups would feel if I drowned. Of course I was trying to get their attention, but I also loved the clean loud splash and then the muffled silence, the perfect solitude underwater.

Long before Chuck and I started dating, I told him how much I hated being around kids.

"I can't imagine teaching grade school," I said. "I'd die if I had to spend a whole day with crying children. I'm never going to have kids."

Chuck seemed amused by my candor. "I wouldn't necessarily want my own, either, just because I like working with them as a teacher," he said.

I was so set against having children that the two of us never discussed the possibility. After we'd been married for more than a year and people asked us why we hadn't yet become parents, Chuck answered, "My wife doesn't even like other people's kids. No couple should become parents unless they're both committed."

If the person who asked the question seemed unconvinced, I added, "My mother was never happy as a stay-at-home mom. She would have wanted me to do something different."

Whenever I had to sit next to a baby on a plane or talk to a friend whose children kept interrupting, my head felt like a hollow eggshell. If the children grabbed my hand or touched my hair, it took all my effort to move out of reach politely instead of recoiling and pushing them away. Once, while I was waiting for a friend to pack a picnic lunch and her two-year-old daughter kept pulling the bottled water out of the bag and throwing it onto the kitchen floor, I pictured myself taking the bottle out of the child's hand

and telling her she was being unbelievably stupid. I made a lame excuse about having to re-pack my car and ran out of the kitchen.

As the door closed behind me, I remembered Hiroshi at the train station on our family vacation. By the time he lost his temper at the man who cut in front of us in the ticket line, my father had endured the whole morning with Jumpei and me. That man was only the last straw. Hiroshi couldn't stop yelling because he was furious to be stuck with us. Years before that vacation, my brother used to wake up in the middle of the night to cry. From my room next to his, I could hear Takako running upstairs to check on him, Jumpei stopping for a few minutes only to start up again, then loud footsteps below and the front door slamming shut. My father didn't come back for days. He claimed he had stayed at a hotel, as though it made any difference where he spent the night when he walked out on his family.

I didn't refrain from having children to avoid my mother's unhappiness. It was my father I was afraid of becoming.

The word *spinster* once referred to anyone—male or female—who spun yarn for a living, but in the middle ages, when the job fell to the unmarried daughter left at home, the word came to mean "an unmarried woman of a certain age." A woman with children, even if she never had a husband, is never referred to as a spinster. Spinsters are supposed to be quaint and fussy, with a lot of time on their hands. With no children to raise, I was more of a spinster than anyone. I could devote hours every day to old-fashioned hobbies like spinning and knitting.

The rugged yarn I spun suited the sporty seamless sweaters, and I could make adjustments for the yarn's unevenness in my knitting. After making a few solid-colored sweaters, I had enough odds and ends of hand-spun yarn to make Fair Isle hats, socks, or vests. When I first started knitting, I had been drawn to the almost mindless repetitiveness of the activity. With one-color knitting, there was little to pay attention to except an occasional increase or decrease. Once I became more adept, though, I enjoyed the added challenge of Fair Isle knitting. While holding two or three skeins in my hands and interlacing the strands after every few stitches, I had to read and follow the marks on the graph paper that showed where each color should go. On the chart, I covered all but the row I was working on, to avoid getting confused. At first, I stopped after every row to make sure that it matched up with the previous row and the pattern was aligned correctly. But most patterns are symmetrical, so once I completed a few rows, I sort of *knew* what color was coming next without looking at the chart. Mastering a Fair Isle pattern was like learning a song or memorizing a poem. I looked at the chart mostly for the pleasure of discovering that I was right. Row by row, I proceeded with a *zing* of recognition as I followed the pattern I could recite by heart.

A YEAR AFTER WE EXCHANGED our lessons, Sharyl quit her job and moved back to Colorado, where she enrolled in divinity school to become a Methodist minister. Before she and Bob left, she talked me into signing up for a week-long weaving class at the school in Northern Wisconsin where she'd gotten her start. "Think of all the things you can make with the yarn you've been spinning," she said. "You'll have a blast." Like those for Fair Isle knitting, weaving patterns featured repeated sequences marked on graph paper. Taking the class seemed like a logical extension of my repertoire.

The weaving school was on Washington Island, off the northern-most tip of the Door Peninsula, which sticks out into Lake Michigan like the thumb of a mitten. Getting there from Green Bay, the base of the thumb, required a two-hour drive on a two-lane highway, a choppy half-hour ferry ride, and a twenty-minute drive across the heavily wooded island. Though the island was a summer resort, most of the vacationers had summer cottages so there were only a few motels and restaurants. The weaving school, housed in old farm buildings, had its own dorm. You couldn't get off the island after the last ferry left at six every night. Had it been easier to leave, I might have.

Weaving involves interlacing two sets of threads at right angles. The vertical threads, called the warp, are placed on the loom first; the horizontal threads, the weft, are added one pass at a time. Securing the warp onto the loom requires a lot of math, planning ahead, measuring and cutting, counting and tying. The first three days of our week-long class were devoted to this process. For the scarf I chose for my project, I had to determine how many warp threads to put on, how long those threads should be, in what color and pattern sequence, and how far apart they should be spaced. The scarf would shrink ten percent in length and five percent in width. The dent—the thread-spacer on the loom that looks like teeth—had twelve spaces per inch, but the thick wool I was using would look better if I used only eight threads per inch. This meant not pulling a thread through every space, but how many to skip and at what interval? I was stuck inside a real-life story problem.

I hadn't minded when the yarn tangled and broke on my spinning wheel, because I could throw it away and start over. The warp couldn't be changed once it was on the loom, pulled through its various parts and tied in place with square knots. If I didn't measure, calculate, or count enough threads, my scarf would have to be shorter or narrower than I'd wanted. If I didn't like the color sequence of the warp, I wouldn't be able to reverse them. If I skipped a thread, there would be a hole. A weaver can work with either thread or yarn depending on what she's making (thread for a table runner or a linen napkin; yarn for a scarf like I was making), and yet, in the process of preparing the loom, the material is always referred to as "thread." Unlike knitting and spinning, weaving requires precision.

Sharyl, who gave up on knitting after three days, was an ultimate "thread" person. I remembered how organized she had been when we exchanged our lessons: she had divided hers into three parts and prepared a handout. Sharyl had loved weaving from the start. The detailed step-by-step instruction that was driving me crazy had suited her. Precision calmed people who were precise by nature. As I looked around the room, most of my classmates appeared busy but serene as they followed the meticulous instructions of our teacher, a heavy-set woman in her fifties who worked as a home-economist in a small town in Michigan, answering questions for the town's "home-making hotline." She knew exactly how many cups of blueberries went into every nine-inch pie.

The ten women in the class were teachers, social workers, store owners, and homemakers from Wisconsin, Illinois, and Indiana. I became friends with Holly, the only other woman who was having trouble. Her knots came undone and her threads tangled. "Right over left and then what?" we kept asking, unable to tie a square knot. Holly taught physical education at a high school, coached track, and rock-climbed and kayaked with her teen-age sons while her husband—an elementary school teacher like Chuck—stayed home to read. At forty-two, she still looked like the gymnast she used to be in college. In her black yoga pants and white T-shirt, her long blond hair tied back in a ponytail, she started each day with an hour-long tai chi routine. Then she made huge buckwheat pancakes in the dorm's kitchen and shared them with anyone who walked in.

After the day-long instruction, Holly and I cooked a vegetarian dinner and took a long drive to watch the sunset instead of going back to the studio to weave as our teacher had recommended. On the west side of the island, there was a private beach with a sign that said, "Pattersons. Family and friends welcome." "Friends, that's us," Holly said as she drove her station wagon past the rocks that marked their property. The Pattersons must have been away. No one came to chase us off their land, so we kept going back. Every night, the sun dropped into the water in a dramatic splash of red and purple, all the more thrilling because we were watching it where we weren't supposed to be.

Once the warp was on the loom, putting in the weft was easy and relaxing, like knitting, spinning, or running: the same motion over and over, keeping the tension right. I had envisioned the scarf as a study of blue and grey and brought enough yarn. The warp I'd put on featured alternating shades of the two, and I started weaving more of the same into the weft. After a few inches, though, the scarf looked bland. The colors were too similar to show off the her-ringbone pattern. Unlike the warp, the weft can be modified as you go along. I went to the yarn store attached to the school and bought small skeins of rose, purple, red, and hot pink, just enough to put in a few passes after every couple of inches. The extra colors made the various blues and greys stand out more.

Holly and I fell further behind after we discovered a good ice cream stand on the island, where we took long midday breaks in addition to our sunset viewing jaunts. I had to stay up on the last night to finish my scarf, because I wanted it long enough to wind around my neck. Holly went to bed earlier, having decided that hers could be the type that tucked in under the coat. After mid-night in the weaving studio, the only noises came from the shuttle I threw across the loom, the beater I brought forward to press against the fabric, the fluorescent lights that buzzed overhead, and the hundreds of small moths and gnats throwing themselves against the window screen. I finished the scarf at four.

On the loom, the fabric gets rolled around the beam, leaving just a few inches of the work in progress in front of the weaver. You can't see the whole pattern until you unroll the cloth at the end. This may be why the suitors in *The Odyssey* didn't notice that Penelope was weaving the same part of the tapestry every day. When I unwound my work, I discovered that the sunsets Holly and I watched had made their way into the scarf. The herringbone pattern had turned into waves of grey and blue; the lines of rose, red, purple, and hot pink were the reflections of the sun. At the final show and tell, I announced that my scarf was titled "Watching Sunsets with Holly Smith," but to myself, I called it the Trespass Scarf.

On the ferry ride back, the pine trees on the island, the sand and pebble beaches, the rocks sticking out of the water, the clouds in the sky, all looked like something we could weave. Holly lived two hours west of Green Bay, so she planned to follow me back to my house on the way back to meet Dorian. He had mellowed with age and only bit people like the vet and Chuck's brother Brian (our reluctant cat sitter), against whom he'd held a longstanding personal vendetta. Holly and I left our cars in the hold and sat on deck, sipping the wine cooler she had hidden in her coffee thermos. When the ferry docked and some of the passengers rushed toward the stairs while the others continued to sit, Holly said, "God, people are so uptight. What's the rush?" We remained on deck, chatting about the highlights of the week. After ten minutes, we suddenly realized that some of the people had hurried away because, like us, they had their cars in the hold. The more relaxed passengers had only themselves to get off the ferry. When we dashed downstairs, the long line of cars parked behind us were waiting to leave. Drivers beeped their horns in annoyance, but we only laughed harder.

Everything I wove after the class, on the loom I mail-ordered from Vermont, had the meticulously prepared part and the break-the-rule, forget-the-car, trespass-for-sunsets part. I made my second scarf from a bag of fleece I divided into batches and dyed in the oven—baked for an hour at 350 F°—with three flavors of Sugar-

Free Kool-Aid: Grape, Cherry, Raspberry. When I finished spinning, the skeins of yarn ran a spectrum from pale pink to dark purple. On the warp, I wanted the dark and the light to alternate with subtle gradations of waves instead of the harsh contrast of stripes, so I taped the pieces of yarn on an index card to try out the colors before I put them on. But once the warp was in place, I chose the weft as I went along, using whichever color looked right at the time. The scarf resembled a sunset over a field of poppies. Wrapped around my neck, it smelled vaguely sweet.

THE WEAVERS' GROUP I JOINED in Green Bay met every month at a different member's house. At seven o'clock sharp, we began our business meeting. First, the officers—the president, the treasurer, the secretary, the historian, the social chair—gave their reports, and then we discussed the items on the agenda we'd been mailed. The topics included which books or tapes to purchase for our traveling library, what color our new group T-shirts should be, and what events we should organize for the art fair downtown and the "heritage day" at the history park (a place with restored old buildings and docents dressed in period costumes, some of whom spoke with a fake French or Southern accent). The meeting was followed by a round of show-and-tell and an hour-long educational program about how to eradicate wool moths, how to identify a mystery fabric by burning a small portion of it and examining the ashes, how to design one-piece garments on the loom. At the end, the hostess served coffee, tea, and homemade dessert.

The spinners' group I'd been attending met at the same community center every month, but people regularly showed up on the wrong night because the fourth Wednesday, our designated meeting night, was not always the last Wednesday of that month. Every time there was an extra Wednesday, the few spinners who went by mistake were surprised to see the bingo players, the League of Women Voters, or the Environmental Action Coalition instead. The spinners' group didn't have officers, business meetings, or educational programs. The room was reserved from seven to ten, and people kept arriving and leaving throughout. All we did was sit around with our wheels, spin, gossip, and do a much less organized version of show-and-tell: "show-and-chat endlessly" for some, "show, don't tell" for others, and for one woman who raised sheep and brought bags of fleece to every meeting, "show-and-sell." Most of the spinners had several hobbies besides spinning and knitting. While the weavers limited themselves to showing the garments they'd woven or the weaving books they found helpful, the spinners brought handmade objects of all kinds even if they didn't include hand-spun yarn or any yarn at all. We were supposed to take turns with the snacks, but people forgot which month they'd signed up for. It was okay to bring store-bought cookies or potato chips instead of homemade pies and cakes like the weavers. The community center had a hot pot for making tea and coffee.

The members of both groups were homemakers, nurses, social workers, teachers, librarians, dental hygienists, dairy or sheep farmers, data processors, and secretaries. Every time we met, twenty to thirty women showed up. The youngest were in their thirties like me and the oldest in their seventies. Many had been at the closing-day sale of the only yarn store in town and remembered the double-parked cars and the incredible discounts; they were still knitting and weaving from those bags of yarn. Everyone had children except Sharyl and me. Sharyl, who used to belong to both groups, was in Colorado by the time I joined the weavers. Most people eventually chose one group over the other. Spinners stopped coming to the weavers' group, because "God, those people were such control freaks." Weavers quit the spinners' group, because "They were so unorganized they made me nervous." When the two groups did joint demonstrations at the art fair, the weavers organized everything, the spinners came late, and everyone complained, but not enough to refrain from trying it again the following year.

I was more comfortable with the spinners, but I kept going to both and even served, one year, as the weavers' vice-president. I was hoping my flexibility would keep the weavers from becoming too rigid, just as Sharyl's discipline had saved the spinners from utter chaos. I didn't understand the paradox that Sharyl's move should have made clear. Sharyl didn't fit in at the college any more than I did. As a childless woman whose husband took up weaving, she, too, felt out of place in Green Bay. While she had managed a cross-country move and a complete career change, I had only added a few hobbies to my routine. Fair Isle knitting and weaving had taught me to follow a few step-by-step instructions, but that wasn't, remotely, enough. I was still working only one row of color marks at a time and hoping that some kind of over-all pattern would emerge by accident or through a miracle.

My haphazard, one-thing-at-a-time approach wasn't flexible at all. On the contrary, I was paralyzed by my inability to make any long-range plans. If I'd had been better organized, I could have updated my curriculum vitae, written my job application letters, and sent them out instead of thinking vaguely about them forever. The big talk Chuck and I kept postponing could have been a problem-solving discussion. Although Sharyl couldn't accept her crooked scarf, she had no trouble making a difficult and messy life change. She had moved on while I remained stuck. The women I met through spinning and weaving were small-town mothers with families to raise. They didn't visit each other's houses or meet at the downtown mall for coffee. I hadn't even made any close friends. Although that was about to change, I could hardly take credit for the improvement.

DURING MY FIRST YEAR at the college, a student who was my age had taken the Modern American Novels class I was teaching. Jim already had an art degree then, but he had joined the Norbertine order as a novice and returned to school for a teaching certificate and signed up for my class as an elective. We'd had coffee and talked about writing and about how he hoped to balance his vocation and art. Five years later, he came back from teaching high school in Chicago to live at the abbey and to serve as the new chaplain of our college. He was now an ordained priest, though in his jeans, T-shirt, and denim jacket, he looked more like the models in a J. Crew catalogue. Over six feet tall, with a mop of blond hair that fell over his blue eyes, he had a warm smile and a quick wit. If he hadn't been a priest, he might have been the most eligible bachelor in town.

Jim thought women should be ordained, the church should support reproductive rights, gay rights, and divorce, and people should be less concerned about the rules and more about true charity. He bought old religious books at rummage sales and library closing sales and wrapped them in silk or crinkled the pages one by one till the whole volume opened up like a big flower. He found antique chalice boxes lined with velvet and placed newspaper articles about human rights violations inside. He was planning a series of embroidered collages about domestic violence. No matter how disturbing the message, his art work was always beautiful to look at. His room at the abbey was covered with the silk kimonos and obi sashes—woven with gold thread—from the antique stores in Chicago. Jim had signed up for a weaving class at his art school but was defeated, he said, by "the mathematics of weaving." He was still interested in needlework. It was as though, in the years we hadn't seen each other, we had discovered the same interests.

Jim and I started having monthly vegetarian dinners in the abbey's guest kitchen with Beth, the new geographer at our college who had dyed her hair carrot red. A single mother and no spinster, Beth dated men she met through the personal ads placed in the *Milwaukee Sentinel*. She'd grown up in a small town on the Minnesota border, spent her twenties in South America doing volunteer work and geographical research, and come back to her home state so her teen-age daughter could finish high school. Beth knew the hidden word on the puzzling sign I saw out in the country, illustrated with a big cartoon rabbit holding red balloons: "Rabbits Live or (a blank space covered with paper to indicate temporary unavailability)." "Not," "Skinned," "Frozen," "Ready to Eat," were the guesses I'd fielded so far, but none of them sounded quite right. "Dressed," Beth said. "My neighbors used to raise rabbits." She hadn't eaten rabbits since she left her home at eighteen. To our monthly potluck, which we called "the Black Sheep parties," she brought lentils and brown rice.

The fourth Black Sheep was Don, a Lutheran minister who taught theology at our college. I knew we were going to be friends when he knocked on my office door one afternoon and gave me a sock doll he'd made with the names of the two faculty members I really hated written in red; dangling from the doll's neck were a dozen pretty cocktail toothpicks to stick into it. "How did you know I hated these people?" I asked. "I've been watching and listening," he said. Like Beth and me, Don had gone to a foreign country to get away from his family. He'd grown up in Pennsylvania but attended college in Germany. His earliest memories included his father walking into their living room in a drunken rage and setting the Christmas tree on fire. "I only remember it like a silent movie," he told us, "even though there must have been a lot of noise when it happened." One of his life's goals was to be a better father to his three young children and a reliable husband to his wife—an energetic, motherly woman who had "minister's wife" written all over her—but he came alone to the Black Sheep party.

What the four of us had in common was an early history of not belonging to anyone or anything. By the time we met, each of us had made a commitment other people could understand: the priesthood for Jim, the family and the Lutheran church for Don, motherhood for Beth, marriage for me. But we all felt like undercover agents in the roles we'd chosen. With one another, we didn't have to pretend or explain. We didn't try to outdo each other with the horror stories of our past. We might even talk about something frivolous, like an obsession with David Lynch's "Twin Peaks" series. Don looked like Kyle McLaughlin, the actor who played Agent Cooper, the show's main character. He was devastated when Agent Cooper became Bob, the evil spirit, in the show's final episode.

"What does that mean about me?" Don said half-jokingly. "I really identified with him."

"Oh, you're not going to turn into Bob," Beth said, patting his arm.

"Not a chance," Jim agreed.

"Agent Cooper was never a devoted Dad," I assured him.

Don shrugged and smiled. Of course he was afraid of turning into his father—for all four of us, the evil spirit was our father, one way or another. We scarcely had to say it. Jim, Beth, and Don were the only people with whom I could be reticent because they already knew—not because they would never understand. Sitting on the roof of the abbey with them and watching the summer dusk fall around us, I thought I had finally found a group of people I wanted to know for the rest of my life.

But Beth and Don had temporary jobs at the college, and when the positions opened up for tenure-track appointments, they weren't even interviewed. After they moved away, Jim and I had dinners out, took day trips to Milwaukee to see art exhibits, or met on Saturday mornings in the fields and meadows outside town to cut the wild flowers he arranged for the sanctuary. Like my child-hood friends—though for an entirely different reason—he had stud-ied Japanese flower arrangement at college. He took the Queen Anne's lace we gathered and mixed it with the peacock feathers a parishioner had given him. The white globes of the Queen Anne's lace and the golden circles of the feathers floated over the altar, like a mysterious model of the universe that was infinite and expanding.

Jim's mother had died of cancer when he was twenty. His father had left the family when Jim was in high school, and later, belittled Jim's decision to join the priesthood. Jim no longer spoke to his father, who was still, like mine, alive. Long before he became a priest, he knew he would never marry or have children. When we were walking around the fields—trespassing again—I could almost believe that the love of beauty we shared was a kind of faith. He was the person I was closest to even among the Black Sheep; still, I missed having a group around us, a fellowship of permanent outsiders.

THOUGH I KEPT GOING to the spinners' and weavers' meet-ings, I was doubly a stranger to these woman by being Japanese and childless. As long as I lived in Green Bay, I thought, this was the best I could do: I felt more at ease surrounded by animals than by humans. I wished Chuck and I lived in a larger house so I could get a dozen angora rabbits to keep myself busy. Rossetti and Frida needed a haircut every eight weeks for their health as well as for my spinning. Unlike a cat's, rabbits' digestive systems are only equipped to handle vegetables, fruits, hay, and alfalfa pellets; ingesting their own long hair could block their intestines and even kill them. There are no long-haired rabbits in the wild. Rossetti and Frida were hybrids dependent on me for their survival. Like all domestic rabbits, they were also prone to respiratory problems. Chuck considered them pathetically high-maintenance, but I loved brushing and cutting their hair, coaxing open Rossetti's mouth to give her medicine when she had a cold, or clipping Frida's ingrown nails. Though they were docile, they didn't crave my attention like Dorian, who slept with his head on my pillow and drank from my bedside glass instead of from his designated bowl on the floor. Chuck and I usually forgot that Dorian was not fully human. Caring for Frida and Rossetti actually made me realize how much I enjoyed working with animals. Since I didn't have space for more rabbits, I went to volunteer at the wildlife sanctuary in our city's parks system.

Handling wild mammals like raccoons and squirrels required rabies immunization—a month-long course of injections with a blood test at the end to see if they even "took," starting over if they didn't. So, I signed up to work with birds and became one of the dozen rehabilitators on call in the summers when concerned citizens brought shoe boxes of baby birds fallen from their nests. In the winter, I helped care for the raptors who lived in the sanctuary's aviaries, because their injuries had rendered them unfit to be released back into the wild. My favorite job was to hold the owls while another volunteer filed down their beaks and trimmed their talons. Most sanctuary volunteers were my age, childless, and vegetarian, and they belonged to other nonprofit organizations in town. Just when I was ready to give up, I had finally fallen in with a group of people who were more like me than not.

As it turned out, in Green Bay, if you were interested in environmental protection, animal welfare, homeless advocacy, women's rights, gay rights, the Quakers, the Unitarians, the psychic church, or the health food movement, you eventually met all the twenty or thirty people who shared your interest. Within a year of attending my first training session at the sanctuary, I had enough friends from these groups to start a weekly movie-watching group. The core consisted of divorced women and gay couples in their thirties. Most had grown up in Green Bay or in the surrounding towns. A dozen of us showed up each week, and no one cared what we saw. Like my mother's needlework group, it was the company we sought.

In the theater, we took up a whole row of seats and were often the only ones there. Pete, my librarian friend, fell asleep and snored every week. After we saw "Fargo," everyone except me claimed that their parents, brothers, or sisters (but never themselves) talked like the characters. The bird watchers among us tried to identify every stray bird that flew across the screen, which drove the others crazy. "Too many tea cups," Tim, an out-of-work mathematician, said about a movie based on a Jane Austen novel. "What a dog," Lori, a pet-store clerk and former English major, muttered after a movie about T. S. Elliot. I thought she was criticizing the movie, but she meant the poet. Afterward, we went to the only pizza parlor still open at nine. The Black Sheep had been the siblings I should have had all along: Jim, Beth, Don, and I might as well have grown up in the same family in four different cities. The movie group was more like a gathering of cousins or neighbors, which some of them, in fact, were to one another; they were an extended family I had married into.

Most in the group knew Chuck, because they had gone to his high school, their children attended the alternative school where he taught, or their friends, siblings, or cousins had dated, worked with, lived next door to, or bought a house or a used car from Chuck's friends, siblings, or cousins. Chuck believed in the same causes that had brought us together. Still, he didn't go to the Audubon Society meetings or the AIDS walks with us, and he came to the movie night only if he was interested in a particular show. While the rest of us drove to the pizza place, he went home alone.

Chuck didn't socialize with anyone he worked with at the alternative school. The only new friends he'd made since high school were his Milwaukee roommate George, with whom he went on an annual camping trip, and me. The group who watched football and played cards with him got smaller every year. "We were never that close growing up anyway," Chuck would mutter about someone he'd stopped seeing, as though it had taken a quarter of a century to figure out who was and wasn't a true friend from middle school. While I'd been working to expand my social circle, he had been trying to make his smaller. If my ideal life was a big Fair Isle sweater, his was a white linen handkerchief.

One of his former roommates had a younger brother enrolled in the creative writing program I had finished. Chuck had known both brothers and their entire family since the seventh grade, but one evening when they called to get together, he handed the phone to me. "Why don't you go by yourself?" he said after the younger brother, Pat, and I made the plans and hung up. "You and Pat probably have a lot to talk about. I'd rather stay home and read."

At the movie group's pizza place, which was their old hangout as well, I told the Moran brothers that Chuck had a cold. I couldn't believe I was making excuses for him to the people he'd known for more than half his life. Once we got talking, though, I was glad I'd gone alone. Pat and I compared our favorite teachers, classes, and books. His brother had been studying fiction writing at the adult outreach center. If Chuck had been there, the three of us wouldn't have felt so free to carry on about the best and the worst writing exercises we'd ever been assigned or the craziest, least helpful suggestion someone made to us in a workshop. We wouldn't have felt the same camaraderie. I didn't care if the strangers at the next table stared at me. I was with friends who understood me.

I didn't have to worry about whether Chuck was having a good time, if he was offended by anything we said, or what he thought of the person I was without him.

⁓

IN THE FALL OF 1992, the stories I had been writing and revising for years finally got published as my first novel. I gave readings at schools, libraries, and bookstores, and the local newspaper ran articles about me. "I saw your picture in the paper," strangers in grocery stores and shopping malls said to me instead of, "Are you Chinese or Japanese?" Although none of them had actually read the book, I was pleased to be recognized as an author instead of a foreigner.

"I can't believe you were working on this all along," my friends from the movie group said. "You were probably thinking some of these amazing thoughts even while we were watching movies together." They shook their heads and smiled; they were so proud of me. "Really, I would never have guessed," they said.

I had only talked about the novel with Jim as we walked around the fields cutting flowers or drove back from an art exhibit in Milwaukee. I had revealed no more to Chuck than to the friends I saw once a week at the movie theater. I gave him one of the advance copies the publisher sent me, but it sat unread for months on his night stand.

"I'm going to start soon," he kept saying. "I just don't have the time right now."

"You don't have to read it if you don't want to."

"But I want to."

"You live with me. You already know me. You don't have to rush to read my book."

I couldn't believe what an insincere remark I was making. The truth was the opposite. Chuck felt betrayed by perfect strangers reading the words I had written and he hadn't read. He didn't know any more about me than they did. But now that I was working on the next project, I had even less desire to talk about my writing than before. Every afternoon, as soon as I finished writing for the day, I wanted to pretend—even to myself—that I was just a school teacher's wife and a small-town college professor instead of a person who'd written an autobiographical novel about grief.

After Chuck read the book, he didn't ask me which things I had made up and which I had actually experienced. He must have hated having to wonder about it, but he allowed me to act as though my writing was "no big deal, it was just a story." It wouldn't have made any difference if he had been angry or brave enough to confront me. I would have gone on telling him nothing, saving up all my true feelings and thoughts for my writing. I didn't know how else to be a writer.

WHILE I WAS LEARNING TO SPIN, Sharyl had given me a drop spindle to practice handling the fleece: drawing out the fiber, letting it stretch, allowing it to twist and turn into yarn. The drop spindle has a metal shaft and a wooden knob. You hold it level with your shoulder, tie a short piece of already-made yarn around the shaft, attach one end of the prepared fleece onto this lead yarn by twisting them together with your fingers, give the knob a good twirl, and let go. If you put just the right amount of spin, the fleece will turn into yarn and the spindle will hang in the air a few inches above the floor, swinging gently. You pull up the spindle by the yarn you just made, wind the yarn onto the shaft, give the knob another spin, and let go again. As you add more yarn, the spindle becomes heavier and drops faster so you have to spin it harder to keep the yarn from breaking. When the spindle is too heavy, you can unwind the yarn into a ball, leaving enough for the lead yarn, and start over. Once you learn the right timing—holding on, letting go—you can walk around your house while twirling and dropping the spindle, or herd your sheep to the grazing ground and back as women in South America and the Middle East still do. I loved watching the yarn spin out like a life line as the spindle glided down.

While I was trying to finish the novel, I had gone back to Japan for the first time to see my grandmother, aunts, and uncles. I'd spent the summer of 1991 traveling around the country and staying with some American friends in Kobe. At last, I was able to talk to my relatives as an adult and hear the stories I'd been too young to know, but as soon as I returned to Green Bay, my trip felt as distant as my childhood—something to write about from the safety of my studio. That winter, as I was driving back in the snow from the spinners' or the weavers' meeting or sitting in the dark with friends whispering and passing popcorn down the row of theater seats, I finally felt at home where I was. After the book was out, I traveled across the state and even the country to give readings and to speak on panels with other writers, but what I liked the most was coming back. My car was a spindle clattering down the highway; the maps in airports reminded me of the wheel, with long threads spinning out of a few hubs and stretching across the continent. Over and over, I was drawing away and pulling back before the yarn broke.

Spending a few days in New York or San Francisco didn't make me wish I could move there. Plenty of other people like me—exiles from other countries—lived in those cities. Being in a small town in Wisconsin was my unique destiny. At last I felt *married* to Green Bay for better or worse, and my marriage to Chuck was the foundation of my ties to the community. As a single woman from Japan, I would have been an outsider even among the divorced women and the gay couples I met. As Chuck's wife, I was almost a local, a member of the famous football family known to everyone. Although he seldom went anywhere with me, Chuck anchored me to the home I'd chosen.

I should have given him the same chance. Visiting the Zen temples in Kyoto had been Chuck's lifelong dream. When I decided to go to Japan, though, I'd said, "I need to do this on my own. I have a lot of people to see and talk to."

"Well, maybe next time," he'd replied, "if you take another trip there."

My grandmother had never spoken to anyone from another country. She was past ninety: of course I wanted to be alone with her. Still, I could have arranged for Chuck to visit Kyoto while I was at her house. I might have introduced him to an American friend who could show him around or signed him up for a meditation class at a Zen temple. But in Japan, even to go somewhere without me, Chuck needed my help. The thought of having to plan his trip as well as mine overwhelmed me. So I left him behind, better to take care of myself. After making him move back to his hometown for my job, I refused to give him even a few weeks in mine. I didn't notice how selfish I was being because leaving people behind was all I had ever done.

ON A SUNDAY AFTERNOON in April of 1993, I was driving back from a reading I'd given in Madison. Halfway home, the air outside the windows suddenly turned white with snow, and the ground billowed like the clouds under an airplane. For a few miles, I couldn't see where the road ended and the surrounding fields began. The squall passed as quickly as it began, though, and the sky cleared into a watery blue. I was in the middle of the state where the land lies low and flat. The road stretched straight ahead and behind, between the bare fields with thin patches of melting ice and snow.

After so many winters in the Midwest, I no longer considered the wide open spaces to be empty or desolate. This was what home looked like to me on that spring afternoon: long bands of brown, cream, and grey under the pale blue sky, patches of snow, a sharp glint of ice. It resembled the first scarf I had in mind to weave, the composition in grey and blue. The colors that had seemed bland on the loom were consoling, even beautiful, in the vista that spread around my car. I had become a part of the landscape I hadn't been born into.

When I arrived back in Green Bay, Chuck would tell me that my father had died. My brother had telephoned earlier that morning and asked me to fly back to Kobe. Hiroshi's death would forever change the way I thought about home. But for now, for another hour, I could watch the road spinning out unbroken behind me.

Pullovers

I N SPITE OF THE HARSH winters, Green Bay was my
refuge from Japan, and sweaters and blue jeans were my
favorite garments. The first sweater I knitted for Chuck was a
denim-blue pullover with beige, white, and cream squares in the
yoke. The pattern, called "Candle-Lit Windows," came from
Nova Scotia, where the average January temperature is 23 F°, the
expected yearly snowfall is 107 inches, and people live in fishing
villages scattered along the coast. The colors were meant to blend
into the winter landscape of early dusk and snow-covered shores.

The blue pullover was the second layer (after the T-shirt) of
the cold-weather ensemble Chuck put on when the temperature dipped below zero. It was followed by a hooded sweatshirt,
a denim jacket, a down parka, and a scarf long enough to wrap
around his face three times. The afternoon we walked to the
grocery store to buy milk, he was wearing all of that plus long
johns under his jeans, a ski mask, three pairs of socks, two pairs
of gloves, and his grandfather's sheepskin hat with the ear flaps
tied under his chin. Our schools were closed, and our cars did-
n't start. The wind chill was minus sixty.

It took us twenty minutes to walk the six blocks we ordinarily drove. The sidewalks were ankle deep in snow from the last
storm. As we stumbled along, the cold air made us light-headed.
No one else was out walking, but several cars were parked in
front of the supermarket with their engines running. The dozen
customers inside were buying the usual emergency staples—
milk, bread, potatoes, TV dinners, canned soup, ground beef,
iceberg lettuce.

On our way home, Chuck had to carry the gallon jug by its
handle, holding it aloft like a camping lantern; we hadn't

thought to ask for a bag. The dry snow swirling around our boots resembled weird, radioactive sand. "We might as well be on another planet," Chuck shouted through his ski mask and scarf. He was moving with the wobbly gait of an astronaut in space. I imagined living on a planet where milk was an all-purpose energy source, both an illumination and a drink. Chuck was laughing. This was the kind of afternoon he longed for on the few days every summer when the temperature hit the 90s.

To accommodate the layers he wore on top, Chuck needed his sweaters to fit snugly. He was nearly six feet tall and only weighed 140 pounds. The blue pullover was perfect until our fifth year in Green Bay, when he turned thirty-five and suddenly gained fifteen pounds. Cashiers at stores stared at him every time he wrote a check. In the driver's license photograph, his eye sockets appeared hollow.

"I wouldn't take a check from this guy, either," he said to the teen-age clerk at a record store. He turned to me and added, "I can't believe I looked like this and you actually went out with me."

"This isn't a very good picture," I said. "I don't think you were ever so pale."

"But I was this thin?"

"Yeah."

He shook his head in disbelief and assured the clerk that his driver's license was authentic. "I wouldn't have chosen such a crummy picture for a fake ID."

I made another sweater for him and reclaimed the blue pullover. It hung off my shoulders and came down to my knees, but I didn't mind. I, too, wore several layers of clothing—a tank top, a cotton turtleneck, a long-sleeved T-shirt, a short-sleeved T-shirt, and another, looser tank top—but they were all under my oversized sweater and down coat. My T-shirts and tank tops were red, orange, green, pink; my coat was purple. Even if I was only walking to my car, I dressed bright and big, as though I could scare the weather into submission. I didn't understand why people described me as "petite" and "tiny" when, in my mind, I was a giant of strength.

⁓

SWEATERS STARTED OUT AS WORK clothes for fishermen in the Channel Islands in the fifteenth century and were adopted by American athletes in the 1890s. Women didn't wear them until 1917, when Coco Chanel introduced the jersey dress: a machine-knit pullover worn as an unbelted dress, draping straight from the shoulders to the hem instead of fitting tightly around the corseted hourglass figure. "In inventing the jersey dress," Chanel remarked, "I liberated the body, I eliminated the waistline." Marcel Proust lamented how "ordinary" women looked without their corsets, but Chanel was undeterred. In 1926, when she was asked to design costumes for Jean Cocteau's play *Orpheus* she dressed the hero in a sweater and slacks. A few years later, she put women in slacks and sweaters to promote a unisex look. Ever since, sweaters have been a staple in a woman's wardrobe—a sporty, no nonsense garment.

Coco Chanel was born in 1883 in a small town in southwestern France. Her father was a peddler and her mother, a shop girl. After the death of her mother, when Chanel was eleven, her father abandoned his three daughters to an orphanage, and Chanel never saw him again. At age eighteen, she went to work as a shop assistant, a seamstress, and a music-hall performer. The first man she lived with, a former army officer and racehorse breeder, installed her in a big house in the country; the second lent her money to open a millinery shop in Paris. She bought hats and re-trimmed them to sell—making them smaller and simpler, because she considered the huge hats of the time to be ridiculous—before she started designing the casual, elegant, loose-fitting clothes she became known for.

Though Chanel had many admirers, including the Duke of Westminster and the Grand Duke Dimitri of Russia, she never married or had children. She insisted that she didn't want to settle down, that even rich women needed to work instead of sitting idly at home. The romantic partners of her youth, before she became a famous designer, wouldn't marry her, because she was a peddler's daughter raised in an orphanage. Arthur Capel, the Englishman who helped her start her business, was already married when they started living together. Though he died in an automobile accident in 1918, Chanel considered him her true love—the person who "made me what I am, developed what was unique in me, to the exclusion of the rest." Her story had something in common with that of Okiyo-san, my father's long-time lover.

───

I DIDN'T KNOW MUCH ABOUT Okiyo-san until after Hiroshi's death when she called my aunt's house, where I was staying, and asked to speak to "Hiroshi-san's sister." I was immediately suspicious: strangers do not address each other by their first names in Japan. The caller should have referred to my aunt as "Mori-san's sister" or "Mrs. Tone."

After they talked, Aunt Akiko said, "That was Okiyo-san, your father's girlfriend."

"Which girlfriend?" I asked. Long before I learned the "facts of life" at thirteen, I'd understood that the women who called our house late at night were Hiroshi's girlfriends. I pictured him walking under the neon signs downtown with lip-sticked women while my mother sat working on her embroidery. From their voices and local accents, I could tell there were several different women.

According to my aunt, Hiroshi had met Okiyo-san at a bar he went to with his friends the year before I was born. Okiyo-san was the bar hostess there, and her husband, who was a sailor, was seldom around. Hiroshi encouraged his coworkers to patronize her bar, because she was his "special friend." He eventually lent her money to buy the bar from the man who owned it. When Takako found out about the loan, Hiroshi told her not to worry—he would never leave our family to marry a bar hostess. "He can't be completely serious about her," Takako said to Akiko, her sister-in-law and close friend. "Other women keep calling him, too. They all sound pretty desperate." My aunt later wished she had understood how upset my mother had been.

Okiyo-san wanted to divorce her husband and marry Hiroshi after Takako's suicide, but Hiroshi chose Michiko, whose mother managed the bed-and-breakfast in Kyushu, the southernmost island of Japan, where he often traveled on business. Okiyo-san must have forgiven him right away. A few months after her marriage to Hiroshi, Michiko came to Akiko's house and cried because Hiroshi was already spending too much time with Okiyo-san.

"I advised her to go home and be patient," Akiko told me after his death. "I wanted to remind her that she, too, was once his out-of-town girlfriend, but what good would that do?"

Hiroshi had fewer affairs as he got older, but Okiyo-san—he confided in Akiko—wasn't just a girlfriend: she was practically his family. A year before he got sick, he gave Akiko a box of peaches Okiyo-san had sent to his office. "I can't take these home," he told her. "You eat them for me, but don't say anything to Michiko." Okiyo-san lived in a town famous for its peach orchards. When my mother was alive, she'd sent the boxes right to our house. That's how I remembered her when Akiko said, "Okiyo-san was your father's girlfriend even before you were born. She lives in Mizushima."

"You mean the woman who sent us peaches every year?" I asked, and Akiko nodded.

When Okiyo-san called during my visit, my aunt thought she was trying to get information about Hiroshi's final days.

Hiroshi had been home till the morning of his death, because there was nothing more the doctors could do for his cancer. Akiko assumed he and Okiyo-san had fallen out of touch as he had gotten sicker. But Okiyo-san interrupted her account and said, "I know. We spoke a few hours before he was taken to the hospital to die. He called me and said, 'I don't have a lot of time left. I know this is the end.' He was breathing so hard he could scarcely speak." Even in the last six months when he was bedridden, Hiroshi had called Okiyo-san whenever Michiko stepped out of the room. Okiyo-san knew more about Hiroshi's final days than Akiko did, but she was calling to ask a favor. She hadn't been invited to the funeral. She would never be allowed inside Michiko's house to pay respect to Hiroshi's spirits at our family's Buddhist altar or visit his grave on the anniversaries of his death when people gathered to remember him.

"He loved peaches," Okiyo-san told my aunt. "When they're in season, may I send a box to your house? Will you bring a few to the altar at his house and offer them to his spirit?"

"I promised her," Akiko told me. "She didn't leave me much of a choice."

"How would you manage that?" I asked. "If you took a bag of peaches to my stepmother's house, wouldn't she figure out who'd sent them? It's not as though you could just sneak them in."

"I don't know how I'm going to do it," Akiko said, "but I have to try." She shook her head and made a face.

"You could take a few oranges and apples along with the peaches," I suggested, "to avoid being conspicuous."

"Your stepmother doesn't get confused so easily, but I'll think of something." My aunt started laughing. She was going to have to lie for Hiroshi even after his death, but maybe she didn't mind.

COCO CHANEL'S FIRST LOVER, the retired army officer, lived with her openly, because both his parents were dead by the time he met her. He threw parties at his house and introduced her to his friends, but at the horse races they attended every week, she couldn't accompany him to the raised stands. She had to watch from the muddy, grassy area below. While the wellborn ladies perched on the stands in their white dresses and feathered hats, holding ruffled parasols in their gloved hands, Chanel stood alone on the grass in her small boater and long black coat. She came to believe that true elegance lay in simplicity, because, as a kept woman, she could not display herself in public.

It was easy for me to feel sorry for Okiyo-san, who had to grieve for Hiroshi in private. Unlike Michiko, she didn't wrong me directly by becoming my stepmother. Besides, what she told Akiko let me off the hook. Hiroshi had called her everyday — whenever she wasn't being watched by Michiko. He could have telephoned me as well when she wasn't around to discourage him.

Hiroshi and I had seen each other only three times after I left the country — once in New York and twice during my eight-week visit to Kobe. He had never met Chuck or anyone from my adult life. In his last letter to me, a few months before his death, Hiroshi informed me that he and Michiko had sold their large condo and moved to a smaller one so they could easily go to a nursing home in a few years. He said I was too selfish to help them in their old age. He wondered if I ever planned to have children instead of only taking care of myself. "What is the point of living such a selfish life?" he asked. I burned the letter without copying their new address so I wouldn't be tempted to answer it. *No, I'm not planning to have children,* I wanted to say. *Your legacy doesn't deserve to be continued into the future.* I had no idea he was sick, much less, dying. He was sixty-six.

KYOKO MORI

As was the custom in Japan, Hiroshi wasn't told about his cancer, so maybe he didn't know he was dying, either. The doctors had shared their diagnosis only with Michiko, who told Akiko and Jumpei and made them promise not to contact me. Hearing from me, she insisted, would only upset Hiroshi. Jumpei telephoned the day after Hiroshi's death and asked me to come to Kobe for a week. On the flight, I kept wondering what Hiroshi and I might have said to each other if we'd known the truth. A part of me wanted to believe that Michiko had kept us from having at least one honest conversation. Okiyo-san's story put an end to this sorry delusion. My father had plenty of time to say his last words to the people he cared about. I wasn't one of them.

A COUPLE OF YEARS BEFORE my father's death, a friend from my high school had decided to get married at thirty-four. Nobuko had gone to college in Switzerland and gotten a job in Kobe as a regional manager for an international company. After she resigned her position, her full-time job was preparing for her *omiai*. She and her mother went through the stacks of dossiers the marriage broker took to their house, met with numerous candidates, and in the end, chose a widower who worked at a trading company. Her marriage made me wonder why my father had not gone to a professional matchmaker after my mother's death. Every candidate available to Nobuko was a widower in his forties or fifties; most had children. A woman in her thirties was considered lucky to marry at all. My father had been so concerned about our family's reputation after my mother's suicide that he bribed the police and the newspapers to report that she had died from an accidental gas leak. Then, two months after my mother's funeral, he started living with his girlfriend from a bed-and-breakfast.

Before I knew Okiyo-san's story, I had assumed that Hiroshi had been too infatuated with Michiko to care what people thought. Between his shock about my mother's suicide and his desire to be with Michiko—I'd imagined—he'd lost his head and chosen a hasty marriage. That didn't explain how quickly he started staying out all night, leaving Michiko at home with my brother and me, but I concluded he was fickle. Now I wondered if Hiroshi had married Michiko so he could go on seeing Okiyo-san. Instead of losing his head, he had coolly calculated that his friends, who would shun him for marrying a divorced bar hostess, would most likely tolerate his settling for a single woman whose mother ran a business. Michiko was in no position to object to his infidelity. If Hiroshi had married someone like my friend Nobuko and cheated on her, her family would have gotten involved. An educated woman who married late was likely to have parents who supported her no matter what. They might have advised her to divorce him and come home. He was safer with Michiko. With her, he didn't even have to keep my mother's suicide a secret.

My father must have been surprised when his new wife didn't put up with his affair as easily as Takako had. No matter how upset she got, though, Michiko couldn't stop him from seeing Okiyo-san or doing whatever he pleased once he was away from home. She couldn't leave him any more than my mother could: she had nowhere to go. All the same, when he came home late from a bar or from a supposed business trip, Michiko was often waiting in our living room with her suitcase packed. She didn't ask him where he'd been or with whom. Instead, she told him I had made her so miserable she had no choice but to leave him. She complained and cried till he slapped my face, grabbed me by the hair, and pushed me down on the floor to beg her forgiveness. I knew, even back then, that I didn't deserve to be treated this way: Hiroshi was sacrificing me to keep his freedom.

ONE OF THE POPULAR CHILDREN'S stories Takako told my brother and me was about Momo Taro, the Peach Boy. Momo Taro sprang out of a giant peach that came floating down the river where an old woman was washing her laundry. The old woman and her husband, who had no children, raised him as their own in their humble cottage. When he grew up, Momo Taro went to an island where the horned monsters called *oni* were living. He subdued the *oni*, brought back their treasure hoard and presented it to the local lord, and became a hero.

My brother and I wondered how Momo Taro could have recruited his helpers—a dog, a monkey, and a pheasant—with the millet dumplings the old woman had made for his lunch. The pale green dumplings, sold at the train station near Momo Taro's legendary hometown, glittered from the sugar sprinkled on top. They were so sweet, probably no dog or pheasant would eat them, though maybe a monkey would. After a neighbor's dog bit me for trying to feed him the peanut butter sandwich from my lunch, Jumpei and I became skeptical about the dumpling story, but we didn't think it was odd for Momo Taro to be born from a peach. In the pictures from before our birth, Takako's stomach looked like a giant peach, so we imagined ourselves curled up inside, waiting to be born. What Hiroshi had to do with any of this, we never thought to question. As far as we were concerned, everyone was born from a peach.

AS A CHILD, my brother played with the kids in our neighborhood while I rode the city bus to visit friends across town. I took English lessons from our American neighbor, but Jumpei was too timid to come along. I was four years older than he, so it was only natural for me to be more confident. Still, our relatives, teachers, and neighbors commented on how shy he was compared to me, and instead of defending him, I made fun of him. After our mother's death, we seldom talked even though we lived in the same house for eight more years. He was sixteen when I left.

We didn't write to each other or speak on the phone till a month before he came to visit Chuck and me in Green Bay. By then, at twenty-seven, Jumpei was a world traveler. He had worked as a movie extra in Australia, hitchhiked through the Middle East, waited tables at a Japanese restaurant in New York, guided tour groups in L.A., and started an import company in Tokyo. He was in South America buying rugs, sweaters, jewelry, and knickknacks for his business partner to sell in Japan. He sent a postcard from Ecuador asking if he could stop in Green Bay to see me before flying back to Kobe to spend a few months with Hiroshi and Michiko.

"All I want," he told us a few hours after his arrival, "is to make enough money so I can keep traveling. I don't like staying too long in one place." Because the technical college he'd attended didn't have a good language program, he had learned English and Spanish from language tapes and private lessons.

Jumpei showed us the slides of his travels: pink flamingos in South America, a woman in a chador in Saudi Arabia, his friends in a desert in Australia. He laughed about how lax the American immigration laws were. The last time he was in the States, he had entered on a tourist visa, worked illegally on both coasts, stayed several months after the visa expired, and yet he was allowed back a year later with no questions asked. I'd had nightmares my last year in graduate school about the visa problems I would have if I didn't find a teaching job. My brother had worked at a sushi place in the East Village and chatted freely with the customers, any of whom could have been an immigration officer. A person who didn't care to stay in one place had nothing to lose. How he became this carefree lawbreaker and I a small-town homeowner and English teacher, I didn't understand—until he started talking about our father and stepmother.

"After I graduated from college, my father got me a job in Tokyo through his connections, but I quit in three months," Jumpei said to us as we sat drinking coffee in our living room. "I had to give up the apartment I was renting and go home. Every night, my father threatened to kick me out if I didn't find another job soon. After a month, he stopped speaking to me. I didn't want to talk to him, either, so that was fine. But my mother couldn't stand being in the middle. She told my father that I was going to do whatever I wanted to anyway so he might as well accept it." Jumpei tipped his head back and laughed. "My mother persuaded him to give me money to go to Australia, because she knew how much I wanted to travel."

My mother, Okasan, he said over and over in two languages, referring to Michiko.

"Do you remember our mother at all?" I asked.

"No." He shook his head. "*Okasan* is the only mother I remember. I wouldn't know what to do without her. I owe her everything."

"That's not what Kyoko thinks about your stepmother," Chuck said.

"I know my sister didn't get along with my mother," Jumpei answered. "But my mother was good to me. I'm closer to her than I am to anyone." After a few seconds of awkward silence, Jumpei changed the subject. He was careful to look only at Chuck when he declared how much he loved Michiko.

Jumpei had brought back a suitcase full of hand-knitted sweaters from Bolivia, dark pullovers with bright geometric designs in the yoke. He spread them on our living room floor and asked Chuck and me to choose one each to keep. The zigzag patterns—red, green, blue, yellow—ran from one sweater to the next like the mazes in our childhood board games. In all the years we played together before our mother's death, I hadn't lost one game of strategy on purpose just to humor him. I was pleased when people seemed disappointed in him for not being as smart as I was. Later, on the nights Hiroshi came up to my room and dragged me downstairs to apologize to Michiko, Jumpei must have been terrified. His room was across the hallway from mine. Maybe he was standing with his ear pressed to the wall, trying to be ready for whatever happened next. Hiroshi and I didn't consider how Jumpei might have felt when he heard us yelling and crying. We cared only about our own anger.

The sweaters my brother gave us were made from coarse hand-spun yarns that hadn't been thoroughly washed. The particles of vegetation embedded in them irritated our skin so much that, a few months after Jumpei's visit, I filled our bathtub with lukewarm water and dunked the sweaters in. Broken leaves, stems, and loose seeds floated up from between the stitches, and the water turned darker and darker as I rolled and swished the sweaters around. If this were a fairy tale, I would have been brewing a magic potion to bring back my brother, to make him forget the past, and to give him a different childhood in which I had guided him out of the woods where we were lost together, abandoned by our parents. But it was much too late for that fairy tale. Jumpei didn't need me. He was more comfortable talking to my cat, who bit him, than to me. The sweaters took days to dry, and even afterward, they turned our wrists and necks pink. Chuck and I put them away and never wore them again.

TAKAKO HAD BEEN THE OLDEST of six children. She was planning to attend medical school after the war, but when her family lost their land in the farm reform, she had to go to work as a secretary to support her younger siblings. Her sisters did the same after they graduated from high school, while two of their brothers went to college. The boys had scholarships, part-time jobs, and whatever money the family could scrape together for the tuition. Shiro became a college professor, and Kenichi a high school teacher. My middle uncle, Yasuo, didn't attend college only because he hated school. Shiro said my mother and her sister Keiko were smarter than he or Kenichi so they should have gone to college, but there had been no scholarships or campus jobs for women.

Although my mother often reminded me to be patient with Jumpei, she only scolded me half-heartedly when I wasn't. She knew my advantage over Jumpei was temporary. That's why she sent me to private lessons—English, calligraphy, piano, modern dance, water color—by myself. "Your brother will have plenty of opportunities later," she explained. If I had stayed in Japan, my father wouldn't have gotten a job for me in Tokyo or paid for me to travel alone to Australia. Instead, he would have gone to see an *omiai* broker and found me a husband from "a good family." My wedding would have taken place a few months after my college graduation, before I had time to find my own apartment or a job to support myself. For a woman from an upper-middle-class family like ours, education only proved that we had good, intelligent genes to pass on to our children.

No one in our family was surprised by how adventurous my brother had grown up to be. He was a modern-day Momo Taro. He traveled all over the world speaking three languages and collecting treasures, while I stayed home with my writing and knitting. I wouldn't have lasted a day in the places where Jumpei traveled, sleeping on the dirt floor of strangers' houses or in a hammock pitched on crowded ships. My brother could tough it out in the world, because he had a home to go back to and a "mother" who supported him no matter what. It wouldn't have made any difference if I had gotten along better with Hiroshi and Michiko. I was only a daughter; he was the son.

EARLY PROFESSIONAL KNITTERS were mostly men. In the medieval cities, only men were allowed into the guilds that controlled the licensing of handcrafts. In the countryside, men as well as women made mittens, hats, and socks to sell during the winter months when farm work became scarce. Sailors and fishermen knitted their own sweaters during their long voyages. But today, amateur and professional knitters are predominantly female.

One well-known exception is Kaffe Fassett, who studied painting at the Museum of Fine Arts School in Boston before moving to England. He shied away from needlework until he was twenty-eight, not because he was a man, but because he believed that serious artists did not dabble in the crafts. Then he "finally succumbed" to the colorful yarn he found at a fabric mill he visited with friends: he bought twenty skeins of yarn and a pair of needles. His first sweater, a striped cardigan he started on the train ride home (one of his friends gave him a quick lesson), used all twenty colors including peach, aqua, black, and turquoise. His books are organized around motifs (stripes, diamonds, stars, flowers, etc.) rather than garment types. He favors unisex pullovers, cardigans, jackets, and vests—simple squared-off garments like canvases—that he can "paint with wool."

Fassett's first book, *Glorious Knits*, was published in 1985. Every serious knitter I met in the late 1980s had a copy. Far more esoteric is the 1972 pamphlet by Dave Fougner, *The Manly Art of Knitting*, with a cover photograph of a young cowboy knitting on horseback. The flyleaf shows a bare arm grasping a needle that looks more like a barbecue skewer. The patterns are for a dog blanket ("Start by knitting something for someone uncritical"), a ribbed cap, a wall hanging, a horse blanket, and a hammock made from rope, using shovel handles or pool cues for needles. According to the pamphlet's author biography, Fougner lived on a ranch in California and bred horses, flew an airplane, sold real estate, played tennis, and "relaxed in the evening with a pair of wooden knitting needles and a skein of yarn."

I envied the exuberance with which Fassett and Fougner tackled every project. Like my brother, they did what they wanted and reveled in their eccentricity. No woman who defied conventions ever seemed so happy-go-lucky.

⁀

THE ONLY MALE KNITTER I KNEW in person was the best poetry student I'd ever taught, and his name, like Fougner's, was Dave. Dave knitted a scarf for himself while he sat in the living room of his fraternity house where one of his roommates was distilling lettuce to see if a person could get high from it. Their fraternity, Kappa Chi, promoted "open-mindedness" (to what, they didn't say). When the poet Maria Gillan visited my class and asked each student to write a poem whose first line was "The mother/The father I wanted would have . . . ," Dave described his imaginary mother playing the saxophone in the garage, the notes bouncing off the concrete walls and floating up to the sky as she takes a funny, self-deprecating bow and smiles to herself—while his real mother sat in the living room reading home-decorating magazines. The silence Dave portrayed was the opposite of the yelling and the crying my brother had hidden from at eight, but Jumpei, too, might have longed to hear one of us playing a saxophone solo in the garage, lost in beauty.

Dave had attended a private high school in a college town. By the time he took my class, he was well beyond the sing-songy rhymes most of my beginning students wrote. But my best fiction student started out as my worst. Rob was a hockey player from rural Wisconsin—a trouble-maker and a straight-A student. When he signed up for my fiction workshop, his sophomore year, he was about to be kicked out of his dorm for starting a fight and vandalizing a parking lot sign, but he'd been hired as a tutor in the writing center and a research assistant for one of my colleagues. In the first two stories he wrote, everything happened only to illustrate an obvious point. Rob had an eye for a quirky detail and an ability to turn a good phrase, but he didn't know how to take advantage of his talent and he hated being told what to do. He was a big kid with a crew cut. The room we met in had tiny chairs with writing pads attached to the arm. The longer Rob sat silent in one of these chairs, the redder his face got. By the time he started his rant about how much he disagreed with me, even the tips of his ears were bright pink. I let him talk because arguing with him seemed pointless.

Rob came to my office one late afternoon toward the end of the semester and said, "I need to talk to you." He slouched in the doorway in his hockey sweats and sighed loudly.

We'd already had several tense discussions over the two stories he'd turned in. Though I asked him to have a seat, I couldn't have sounded too welcoming.

"I've been wrong all this time," he said as soon as he sat down, facing me across my cluttered desk.

"Wrong about what?" I asked.

"Everything," he said, shaking his head. "I went to see my girlfriend in Minneapolis this past weekend and we went running. Halfway through the run, there was a big hole in the sidewalk with an orange cone next to it. Neither of us wanted to let the other go first, so we started running faster. When we were maybe five steps away from crashing into the cone, I thought, 'This is a moment of epiphany, with a hole in the ground, an orange cone, and two people trying to run each other off the road.' My girlfriend and I had no future together. I finally understood what you'd been saying in class. An important moment is also ordinary. I'm sorry I've been such a jerk all semester."

"You haven't been a jerk," I said and he laughed, because we both knew I was only being polite.

⌒

BEFORE HE GRADUATED WITH an English major, Rob took two more writing classes with me as well as an independent study. In the stories he wrote after his "epiphany about the epiphany" as he called that moment with the hole in the ground, a grocery store clerk corralled the shopping carts in the parking lot and dreamed of traveling out west, or a young married couple who ran a lawn care service—like Rob's family did—fought about the husband overcharging one of his customers. I remembered Rob's stories whenever I drove through the small towns in Wisconsin. I expected to run into his characters at some gas station off the highway. While Dave went to the Iowa Writers' Workshop and moved to San Francisco with the poets he met there, Rob took a job as a traveling salesman for the company that installed floors in—among other places—Starbucks. Whenever the company sent him to New York, Boston, or Chicago, he asked for an extra day to visit museums so he could continue his education on his own.

The women who came to small Catholic colleges like ours were better students than the men. Most planned to teach grade school or high school. A few went on to study law or library science. All expected to marry and have children. If there was one thing these women were dying to know, it was how they could pursue a career and still raise a family. They didn't want to study poetry or write short stories or be anything like me, a childless writer. The students who took creative writing were mostly men who belonged to the "open-minded" fraternity or played hockey and soccer and had no idea what they wanted to do in the future. Dave and Rob had good grades, but the others had been sliding through school with B's and C's. When they started writing, they were surprised by how much they actually cared.

Rob, Dave, and their friends (the kid who was distilling lettuce to get high was also one of my favorite students) were as quirky and over-the-top as Kaffe Fassett and Dave Fougner. If they had been professional knitters instead of writing students, they would have used twenty colors in their first sweater and sharpened pool cues into needles to make hammocks. They came to college without a plan and left to do something they hadn't imagined before—which was what my brother had done, too, when he taught himself two languages and set out to see the world at twenty-three. While I resented Jumpei for his freedom, I championed my students. I gave them advice and defended them when they got into trouble with my colleagues, the college, even the local police. I wrote them recommendations, lent them books, and took them to museums. They gave me a chance to be the big sister I'd failed to be for Jumpei. Even so, I was only helpful to them by luck or default. It was Rob's honesty, not mine, that ended our stalemate. My father was right: I was only interested in taking care of myself. Hiroshi and I understood and hated each other's selfishness because we were alike, though I didn't allow myself to consider that until he was dead.

IN THE DIARY MY MOTHER BEGAN in October of 1967, she described how dark and drafty our house was. She wrote once or twice every week, noting the gloomy winter landscape—the bare trees stabbing at the sky, the shadows angling across the road, our neighbors' houses with their windows shut tight. In every entry, her dread of the cold seemed inseparable from her belief that she had wasted her life. Then in mid-March, she suddenly stopped writing. For the next seven months, there was only one short paragraph in July about the flowers and the vegetables in the garden, how the lettuce was growing faster than we could eat it. She must have thought her mood had lifted for good. When she began writing again in October of 1968, however, her misery had returned worse than ever, and she anticipated that every year from then on would be the same. The following March, she only felt strong enough to kill herself rather than wait helplessly for the whole cycle to begin again. She left the diary on the kitchen table, next to the letters she'd written to my father, grandparents, and me.

Nine years later in Rockford, we had so much snow the city was declared a federal disaster area. As I sat in my dorm room with the windows buried in the snow banks, I remembered my mother shivering at the kitchen table. She had stayed wrapped in her quilted bathrobe all day, too depressed to step outside or move around the house. My dorm room was dark at 4 P.M. I got up from my chair, put on my swimsuit and then practically all the warm clothes I owned on top of it, and trekked across campus. "Swim at your own risk," the ID-checker at the door warned. "The lifeguard didn't show up. You're the only person in the building." I was a mediocre swimmer and my eyes burned from the chlorine, but I was so grateful to be moving through that murky, barely heated water.

Takako had written in her diary only in the winter. In the summer when she was happy and active, she had nothing to record. In college and graduate school, rereading her diary and then reading Sylvia Plath and Anne Sexton—women my mother's age, each with two children she left behind when she chose to die—I remembered a Japanese fairy tale Takako had told me about a desolate village in deep snow. Once upon a time, it went, a young farmer in the north country found a small crane shot down on the side of the road. He pulled out the arrow, nursed the bird back to life, and set it free. A few days later, in the middle of the season's first blizzard, a beautiful young woman appeared at his door. She said she'd grown up in a far-away village and her parents, like his, were dead. The young farmer fell in love with her and married her. That winter was one of the harshest. After the couple had eaten their last handful of millet, the wife set up a loom in the shed and wove a beautiful white cloth for her husband to sell in the nearby castle town. Once the food he bought with that money was gone, she wove another cloth, and shortly after, spring arrived. The villagers, out planting their rice paddies, noticed that the young farmer had gotten married and he was not as destitute as before.

When a neighbor asked him about it, the farmer told him about his wife's weaving. The neighbor promised to get a better price for him, if only he could come up with another cloth.

The wife, who had grown weaker with each weaving, had warned him that the second cloth was the last she could weave. But the husband begged till she reluctantly agreed. She made him promise—as before—that he would not come near the shed where she was working. She stayed secluded for two days and two nights. When the loom fell silent toward dawn, the husband went to the shed and cracked open the door. As his eyes adjusted to the dim light, he spied a small, sickly crane tearing out her feathers with her beak and adding them to the cloth. The crane turned back into his wife and told him he had once saved her life. She had hoped to remain with him forever, but the third cloth had taken too many of her feathers. She flew away to die while the husband cried in remorse.

I used to think my mother, with her sewing and embroidery, was the crane wife. My father had betrayed her just as surely as the farmer had his wife, but her diary, more than her needlework, was the crane's weaving. Neither a single entry she made in her diary nor a single poem of Sylvia Plath's or Anne Sexton's released them from their suffering. Their desire for death increased the more they wrote about it: they were tearing out their feathers and weaving them into the cloth, trading their chance for happiness for the words on the page. Plath and Sexton were accomplished poets and my mother only wrote out of her despair, but the results—for their lives—were the same. If my mother had gone to see her friends instead of sitting alone with her diary, she might have survived long enough for one of them to get her the help she needed. Becoming a writer seemed like the worst choice I could possibly make if I didn't want to repeat her mistake, but I didn't know how to stop. All I could do was take care of myself while I wrote, even if it meant having less time for other people.

IN TRUTH, I HAD ALWAYS KNOWN how to save myself from my mother's depression. The selfishness I'd inherited from my father was a protection as well as a curse. If Chuck had cheated on me and lied to me, I would have considered him— not myself—a failure. I had already forsaken the country of my birth, leaving my brother to fend for himself. I knew how to keep moving. My father had played rugby till a year before his death. I, too, was an athlete, constitutionally incapable of sitting still long enough to feel bad about myself. The winter after Chuck and I walked to the store for milk, I learned to run even when it was too cold for my car to start. I dressed in layers and ran around the park near my house, repeating the same half-mile loop so I could stop any time. Snow crunched under my feet and tiny crystals of ice formed on my eyelashes, magnifying the weak winter light. I was my own heat source; I imagined myself as a meteor blazing through space. The physical exercise was only a fringe benefit and not the main point. I had to be moving even while I was sitting at my desk.

Knitting had taught me to plunge into color and swim through it, each row of stitches like a long lap across the pool. Though the motion seemed repetitive, the rows were adding up to a larger design just as the laps were adding to the actual distance I had traveled. My writing, too, had to be a movement and not a repetition. If I could match the perfect knitting tension in my head—holding on and letting go at once—then the words and the sentences sometimes veered away from where they were going and guided me to a new thought that surprised me. I found myself suddenly on the other side of the muddled, tangled phrases, with words for what I didn't know before. Those were the moments to write for. I didn't need to record the same thoughts over and over, no matter how true they had once been. My mother would have written something else in her diary if she had been able. The crane wove three pieces of the most beautiful cloth and nothing else, but that hadn't been her intention: she had meant to stay with the farmer for a long life of happiness. If Sylvia Plath and Anne Sexton had survived their thirties and forties, they would have left a larger body of uneven work instead of a few nearly perfect books. I wanted to write the way I'd been knitting, by trial and error, aiming for endurance. Some projects would turn out better than others, but each would teach me what I didn't know before and prepare me for the next. That's how my life was going to be different from my mother's, how I meant to redeem my father's selfishness into a strength.

BECAUSE I WAS TOO YOUNG to wear my mother's clothes when she died, Aunt Akiko boxed them for storage, saying that I could have them when I grew up. Takako's red and black mohair sweater had fallen on the floor under her makeup stand, where she must have draped it over her chair. I found it while my aunt was packing and hid it in my dresser. After Michiko threw out the boxes, it was the only garment of my mother's that I got to keep.

The sweater, a hand-knitted pullover, has braided cables around the waist and the cuffs. The red yarn and the black yarn were held together and worked as one, blending the colors. There is no label though I remembered it came from a boutique called "Mimosa." Of all her sweaters, this was my favorite because the fuzzy yarn brushed against my cheek when she hugged me. I imagined us turning into bears hibernating in a snow-covered cave where no one would bother us all winter long.

Though I had carried the sweater from Kobe to Rockford, Milwaukee, then Green Bay, it remained in the trunk I used as a bedside table. The day I received news of my father's death, I pulled it out of the trunk, thinking I would take it to Japan and wear it in honor of my mother's memory. I had grown up to be only an inch taller than Takako; we were almost the same size. But as I laid the sweater on my bed with the sleeves spread out, I saw how exquisitely fitted it was—curving in at the waist, rounding out at the bust. My mother's pullover was nothing like the sweaters I made for myself. Takako had been pretty and feminine, a woman who dressed to look small and shapely. She had sat at her mirror every morning, outlining her mouth to resemble a tiny heart, shading her cheeks with the slightest blush.

My mother wouldn't have appreciated my baggy jeans and big sweaters, my plain face without makeup, my refusal to look pretty. If she had lived, we would have argued, like any mother and daughter, about my clothes, face, and hair. We would have suffered through the agony of my separating from her to become who I was. With her gone, I could only imagine the pain and the exhilaration of my rebellion. I was thirty-six. By now, if we had been together, we might have become more like friends or equals finally able to accept our differences. I folded the sweater and slid it back into the trunk. In five years, I would be older than my mother had ever been. I couldn't put myself inside her form. I had to let her be.

— FOUR —

Intarsia

I F I HAD KNITTED CHUCK'S PULLOVER with a plain yoke, he could have worn it even after he gained fifteen pounds, but the beige and the blue yarns interlaced in the back made an extra layer that didn't stretch. In Fair Isle knitting, you always sacrificed flexibility for warmth and durability. The designs were invented for hard-wearing garments like socks, mittens, and workmen's sweaters.

There was another, purely decorative way to knit with two or more colors. For an accent shape against a solid background (a white bunny on a red sweater) or large solid-colored blocks, panels, or vertical stripes, each yarn could be worked in its limited area and left hanging until needed in the next row. In this method, called intarsia, the yarns are lightly twisted together at the color changes to prevent holes; otherwise, they remain separate, keeping the fabric single-layered and flexible.

The ideal marriage Chuck and I had in mind was intarsia: two yarns making their parallel journeys through the fabric, allowing each to cover only its own territory. In the week I spent in Japan after my father's death, I didn't call once to confide in Chuck or ask his advice. How I dealt with my family, I believed, was my business alone.

BY THE TIME I GOT TO KOBE, it was already the third evening after my father's death. I had missed the wake, the funeral, the family ceremony at the crematorium. In the morning, my brother came to our aunt's house where I was staying and said, "*Okasan* is waiting for you. She wants you to pay your respects at the Buddhist altar. I'll walk back with you."

At her house, when Michiko asked me to sign a form to put my father's bank account in her name, I understood why my brother had urged me to come back to Japan. The document Michiko handed me didn't show how much money was in the account.

She was standing at the kitchen counter, with Jumpei, our aunt Akiko, and me seated at the dining room table with our tea.

"This form is so vague," I said. "I don't really understand."

"It's just some legal stuff," Jumpei said with a shrug.

"The paperwork doesn't mean anything," Michiko said, coming back into the dining room to refill everyone's cup. "I don't know why the bank has to bother us at a time like this."

The document wasn't meaningless at all. It was asking me to sign over an unspecified amount of money. Even if I didn't want an inheritance, I had the right to find out what I was giving up.

Michiko hovered over us, still holding the tea pot. Jumpei and Akiko picked up their cups. Neither would glance in my direction. The night before, at the airport kiosk where I'd bought a can of soda, the attendant had put my change on a silver tray, carefully laying out each coin as though it were a gift. I couldn't ask how much money my father had or why the form didn't reveal the sum.

My desire to learn the truth simply to know it, on principle, was so typically American.

I took the pen Michiko had put on the table and signed the form. She said that in the next few days other banks and insurance companies would be sending similar forms. My father had kept his money in so many different accounts. She would bring all the forms before I left the country.

"You don't have to worry about Jumpei," Akiko told me later when we were alone. "Your stepmother has more than enough to live on for the rest of her life, so she's going to take care of him, too."

Though my stay was just beginning, Jumpei left the following afternoon for Tokyo. We walked to the station and said good-bye on the platform where each of us waited for a different train.

WHEN MICHIKO BROUGHT THE STACK of papers for me to sign, my aunt didn't say that I should think it over or consult my husband. People didn't leave wills in Japan. By tradition, when a man died, his widow, oldest son, brother, or nephew inherited everything. A married daughter belonged to her husband's family, not to her own.

I had to sign the forms all the same and officially renounce my claim because by law, only 50 % of the family assets belonged to the widow, with the remaining 50 % to be split equally among the children. The courts didn't care which child was male or female, first-born or second-born, single or married, but the legal division, called *bunke* (breaking the family), was the last resort. If I'd refused to sign the forms and forced my family to follow the law instead of the tradition, even the second cousins I'd never met would have been mortified.

Chuck, too, would have been horrified by my greed. He made snide comments about the one high school friend whose father had been a doctor. When I planned to have dinner at our house with a woman who came from a well-to-do local family, he said I should ask her to coffee so he wouldn't have to get involved. As far as he was concerned, all rich people were snobs or worse. He only made an exception for me, because I'd left home at twenty and gone to school without Hiroshi's help.

If I had called from Japan and told him that I was about to give up 25 % of a sum large enough to support my stepmother for the rest of her life in the most expensive suburb in Japan, he would have cheered me on. But I didn't tell him until I had signed the forms and left the country. When any real-life event was important enough, I treated it like my writing: I could only work in secret, keeping my thoughts to myself. The best way for Chuck to support me was to leave me alone.

I DID RECEIVE A SMALL inheritance from one of the numerous life insurance policies Hiroshi had through his job. For some reason I couldn't understand, the benefits for this policy had to be divided among the three of us instead of paid to Michiko alone. In the eight years I lived with him after Takako's death, Hiroshi had never let me forget that he was sending me to an expensive private school when public education would have been enough for a girl. I hated to be beholden to him even after his death, but the sum was less than what I made every year from teaching. Besides, I already knew what to do with it.

For a few years, I had been spending my summer weekends in Door County, the peninsula I'd first driven through on my way to the weaving school. Situated between the two bodies of water—Lake Michigan and Green Bay—the narrow strip of land had old orchards and dairy farms, meadows, woods, rolling hills, and inland lakes. The vacationers came from Chicago, Milwaukee, or Minneapolis, but the year-round residents who ran the bed-and-breakfasts, art galleries, gift shops, and restaurants had grown up in the small towns across the Midwest. Most of them were single, divorced, married but childless. Just like the movie group in Green Bay, once you knew a few people, you met all their friends.

The person who introduced me to everyone was Norma Jean, who sold hand-made clothes, yarn, knitting supplies, looms, and spinning wheels out of a barn on an old cherry orchard. She was a tall, vivacious woman in her fifties whose grandparents had grown up in Norway. The farm house she lived in, next to the barn, was like a lice-patterned Norwegian sweater in which every space, however small, was decorated. The rooms and the hallways were crammed with Scandinavian furniture, antique lamps, tapestries, quilts, paintings, photographs, doilies and table runners, countless glass dishes and wooden bowls full of trinkets. Next to each chair was a different knitting project Norma Jean was working on.

At the store, as she arranged and rearranged the crowded racks of hand-made clothes, Norma Jean would be trying to knit a scarf, give you a sweater pattern, tell you about her mother's health, teach her Corgi a trick, and wait on her other customers, all at once. She had gone into debt to open two additional stores on the peninsula. Soon after we met, she had to close all three stores, sell the cherry orchard and everything on it, and move to the vacant office of a defunct local newspaper. When the coffee shop she ran out of that space also failed, she went to live in a farm house one of her customers had recently inherited. A friend of ours hired her to hostess at his restaurant. Norma Jean was still designing patterns and knitting sweaters for her former customers. "I'm not organized enough to manage a store," she said. "I don't know why I opened three stores when I could scarcely handle one."

Her landlady was getting ready to sell the farm house and the surrounding twenty acres. Norma Jean couldn't afford the whole parcel, but the landlady agreed to divide the property and sell her the farm house with the five acres around it, if she could help find buyers for the rest. The bank promised a mortgage if Norma Jean could get a cosigner willing to put up collateral. Norma Jean's cousin made an offer on the back ten acres. The eighteen thousand dollars from Hiroshi's insurance was the exact amount I needed to buy the remaining five acres and put them up as collateral to cosign Norma Jean's mortgage. Helping her stay in her new home would get rid of whatever bad karma came with Hiroshi's money. Half a century after my mother's parents had lost their land, I could claim a piece of land whose beauty they would surely have understood.

The five-acre parcel had a stand of maples in the front and an old stone fence in the back. The rest was covered with juniper bushes, meadow grass, wild flowers, and rocks. A mile away, the shoreline with its pines, cedars, and rocks reminded me of the rugged coast of the Japan Sea. As in Japan, people gathered in the small towns on the peninsula to view the cherry blossoms in the spring, the maple leaves in the fall. The tourists didn't stare at me, because they were used to seeing people of color in the big cities they came from, and the locals knew me as a new neighbor. I felt at home in Door County as I had never done in Green Bay.

One of the sweaters Norma Jean had designed, the "Sweater Sweater," was a pullover with five rows of miniature sweaters knitted in the intarsia method across its back and front. Shortly after I bought the five acres, I made mine with leftover yarn from the sweaters, hats, and socks I'd knitted. The miniature sweaters, which alternated arms up and arms down, reminded me of my friends in Green Bay and Door County: a gathering of people who were jumping up and down in some eccentric, out-of-sync celebration.

Placed on the sleeve, above the cuff, was one more sweater each —
a green arms-down crew-neck on the left and a purple arms-up
turtleneck on the right. They were replicas of the sweater I'd given
Chuck to replace the blue pullover and another I'd made for myself.
Depending on how I held my arms, they could be closer together
or farther apart than any other pair on the front or the back.

WHILE CHUCK WENT WILDERNESS CAMPING in Minnesota
and Michigan, I pitched my tent behind the maples on my land.
Since my lot didn't yet have a road, I left my car in Norma Jean's
driveway and hiked to my campsite. Every few weeks, I trimmed
the junipers along the path and cropped the grass under the tent.
Before Door County, I had only gone camping once in college,
on a week-long canoe trip in western Wisconsin. I couldn't stand
the bugs, the poison ivy, the gluey food reconstituted on the Ster-
no stove. Sleeping in a tent in the woods had made me feel closed
in and exposed at once.

In the tent on my own land, I heard the whip-poor-wills singing
through the night and the robins and the cardinals starting up at
first light. One morning before dawn, I woke up to what sounded
like a miniature wind storm. By the time I crawled outside, whatever was making the racket was gone, but later when I described the
noise, one of my friends made a whooshing sound and said, "Did it
sound like this? That's a buck rutting. He thought your tent was a
big animal trying to compete with him." For weeks, I bragged
about how my tent had held its own against a buck.

My new camping experience didn't inspire me to join Chuck
on his wilderness excursions. His favorite spot was on an island in
the middle of Lake Superior. He couldn't imagine sleeping in a
tent pitched on cropped grass fifty yards from a neighbor's driveway, anymore than I could appreciate being dropped off by a "water

taxi" on some deserted shore. When I invited him to come with me, he said no. I pretended to be disappointed, but I was much happier to keep all five acres to myself. Chuck had only seen my land once, from the passenger's seat of my car as we drove by in a rain storm. He admired it at a distance, from his side.

Still, he had understood how I was trying to turn bad money into good by helping Norma Jean. Because Wisconsin was a community property state, he had to sign a form saying he approved my decision to cosign Norma Jean's mortgage. If the bank wasn't satisfied with my five acres, he said, I could add our house to the collateral. Norma Jean had other friends who wanted to help her, but their husbands and wives had refused to let them cosign her loan. Chuck would never have stopped me from doing what I thought was right. That was our pact, to let each other be.

When the two of us had bought our house, I'd thought of owning property as a necessary evil. A part of me had believed that human beings violated the earth simply by existing on it. But now, sitting alone on the stone fence in the back of my lot, I surveyed the meandering paths I'd cut through the junipers and imagined where my house might someday stand. A mile down the road, a woman from Chicago had built a log house from a kit: all she had to do was hire a carpenter to assemble it. Every time I ran and cycled in front of that house, I saw how nicely it blended into its surroundings. Halfway between the maples and the stone fence would be a good spot for mine. I would cut a long curving driveway through the junipers and the rocks, leaving the maples intact. For once, I understood the thrill of having a piece of land I could landscape and reshape to suit me.

Chuck said he would visit my log house when I finally built it, but he himself preferred the north woods, the areas of central and western Wisconsin that were more remote. In Door County, you could get *The New York Times* from the vending machines in front of restaurants; in the small towns in the north woods, all the businesses catered to people who fished and hunted, so even the rare Chinese restaurant served no vegetarian food. Chuck didn't hunt or fish, but he liked hearing the loons calling from the unspoiled small lakes, and he wanted to walk in the woods without running into hikers sporting the latest gear from L. L. Bean. "I wouldn't mind having a summer cottage up north someday," he said.

He was nearing forty, with me a few years behind. We were both becoming less judgmental with age. I no longer thought owning property was evil in and of itself, and Chuck had come to the same conclusion. Like the two panels of an intarsia sweater, I thought, we were progressing side-by-side through the same design.

"It would be great if we each had a summer place," I said.

"Yeah," Chuck agreed. "We should put that in our ten-year plan."

~

BEFORE EITHER OF US COULD build a summer home, we had to address our current living situation. Our house, built in the 1930s, hadn't been redecorated since the 70s. By the 90s, the wallpaper was peeling in every room; the hardwood floors buckled and the paint flaked off the ceiling and the hallways. The concrete steps leading to our front door cracked from the water seeping underneath and freezing. Finally, the mail carrier threatened to report us to the city. He left a note saying he would no longer deliver our mail to the slot on our front door unless we fixed the steps. After a week of no mail, Chuck and I went to the hardware store, bought the letters that spelled out "Mail," and stuck them on the ancient milk delivery chute next to our garage door. We drew a chalk line from the front door, down the sidewalk, and up the driveway. The next day, our mail was in the milk chute and the carrier said nothing more. Once again, Chuck and I were acting like my high school home-ec. cooking team, who had stuffed the over-baked cream puffs through the burned-out holes and called them the "miraculous, ready-to-fill cream puffs: no cutting necessary."

Chuck at least knew how to paint the exterior, from the many house-painting jobs of his youth. The summer after we moved in, he had propped his extension ladder against the west side of the house and started taking off the old paint. He planned to work on one side at a time so the woodwork wouldn't sit exposed too long. If he spent two weeks scraping, sanding, and painting each side, he could do the whole house before school started, but by the time he actually finished sanding the first side, it was mid-July and too humid to start painting. He took a few weeks off, went camping, got busy with other things, and began painting on Labor Day. He couldn't believe his luck: the week after he was done with that one side, in November, the weather turned too cold for the paint to dry properly.

From then on, he set out to tackle one side every summer. He could go around the house in four years, do the windows and the doors in the fifth year, take two years off, and start over again. Houses in our climate were supposed to be painted every seven years.

"We could hire a crew to do it all at once. I'll pay," I offered.

"No," he said. "I like painting. It gives me something to do. I enjoy being outside."

The summer after my father's death, we had been in the house for seven years, and Chuck was just finishing the windows and the trim. The south and the north sides had each taken two summers, throwing him off the original schedule. Already, on the west side, there was water damage that might need re-touching the following year.

"I don't want to start up again next year on the west side," he said one Sunday in late August when I came home from Door County. "Maybe we should move to a new house."

"Because you don't want to paint this one again?"

"No, because I'm tired of living in Green Bay. We should move out to the country."

"I don't know about that. I'm a city person."

"You just got back from Door County. Your summer house is going to have five acres of land around it. Why wouldn't you want the same kind of space the rest of the year?"

My land was a mile from the best restaurant on the peninsula and the auditorium where you could hear Johnny Cash, Michael Hedges, and Suzanne Vega all in one season, but I didn't know how to say that without sounding like a snob.

"Let's just think about it," Chuck said. "We don't have to decide right away."

WE STARTED LOOKING FOR A HOUSE in the country when Dean came back alone from New Mexico in the fall. He had told us on the phone that Katie was planning to join him as soon as she could find a counseling job in the area, but when we showed up at the schoolhouse a week after his return, Dean was weeding the garden with a young girl in a pink frilly dress. The girl's mother was hanging her laundry on the line. A solidly-built woman with blond hair going grey, Jo was wearing an old T-shirt and denim cutoffs. Maybe she was offended by Chuck failing to recognize her as a high school classmate. She retreated into the house, taking her daughter with her but leaving the rest of her laundry for Dean to hang dry.

"We were just driving around," Chuck said when Dean invited us inside for coffee.

"We've been talking about moving out to the country," I added.

Chuck and I stopped at a gas station and bought a newspaper to check the real estate listings, because we didn't know what else to do. Dean was back in the schoolhouse, but we were clearly not welcome there. Looking at property seemed as good a way as any to spend a few hours driving around the countryside. After that weekend, every Sunday when Chuck came home from a football game and I got back from Door County, we got hot-fudge sundaes at the custard stand on the edge of town and hit the county highways. Subdivisions were springing up outside every small town between our house and the schoolhouse. Dean had run into Jo at a grocery store on his third day back, because she was living in one of them. He'd had a crush on her in high school, so he considered their chance meeting to be "fate."

"Dean always went from one relationship to the next, with no break in between," Chuck said one afternoon in late October as we were driving through another subdivision where the houses had the same cathedral windows and rose-colored roof tiles. "It's like he wants to duplicate the exact same life with a different woman."

In several weeks of driving, we hadn't come across one house we wanted to go inside and see. We were heading back home when we saw a handwritten "Lot For Sale By Owner" sign on a ledge. The lot was at the end of a dirt road with a ravine behind it. There were two other empty lots on the same road, but unlike in the subdivisions, the only house nearby was an old farm house with a barn. When we called the number we'd copied from the sign, that farmhouse turned out to be where the owners lived—a couple with one hundred head of dairy cattle, parceling off portions of their land to raise money for retirement. "I was saving that two-acre lot for my niece," the woman said. "We got it zoned for horses, because riding is her hobby, but she got married and moved to Illinois. Why don't you come by next Sunday after church so my husband can take you around?"

Clyde, who met us on the dirt road the following week, was a small man in his sixties with thinning white hair. He must have stopped at home after mass to change—he was dressed in a flannel shirt, jeans, and work boots caked with cow manure. Like my grandfather from years before, he moved surprisingly fast. As he led us down the rocky path toward the ravine in the back of the property, he turned around and held out his hand to me. "I'm fine," I said. "I'm a bird watcher. I'm used to walking on trails." Clyde mentioned the cardinals that came to his feeder and the great grey owls he heard in the trees at night. From behind us, Chuck said, "Kyoko volunteers at the wildlife sanctuary." Clyde said how nice it would be to have benches and bird-watching stands next to the ravine. By the time we climbed back to the road, I'd told him that my other hobbies were knitting, spinning, and weaving, that I had seen llamas at a county fair and thought they might be fun to have around. I would clip their hair, as I did with my rabbits, and make sweaters and hats. "The horse permit we got for my niece-in-law might cover llamas, too," Clyde said. "I'll ask the county supervisor. He goes to our church."

In the woods across the dirt road, the maples were shedding their last leaves. The oaks in the back, slower to change, partially hid the ravine. When all the leaves were down, Clyde said, we would get a clear view of the ravine from wherever we put our house. I remembered the first time Chuck and I had stayed at the schoolhouse with Dean and Katie. We were still living in Milwaukee then, our first spring together. Looking out their kitchen window at the muddy fields, I couldn't believe this was the place Chuck had talked about so fondly. Back then, I'd considered bare trees, pastures with melting snow, and the big open sky to be ugly; I couldn't wait to get back to our apartment in the city. Now I imagined myself walking across my yard to a miniature barn—the kind my spinning friends had built from kits, just like the log house—to care for my llamas. Living out in the country would complete my settling in Wisconsin. It wasn't enough to have a summer cottage in Door County. If

Chuck and I shared a house on this ledge year round, the two sides of my future life would complement each other perfectly.

"You have your writing and your Door County land," Chuck said as we drove back to town. "I need a project, too. You don't have to do anything. I'll be in charge of building our new house."

"But you don't know anything about building a house," I pointed out. "Maybe you should consult an architect before you start."

"I'll get some books," Chuck promised. "I have to fix our house first anyway so we can sell it. That could take a couple of years, but we should buy that land before someone else does."

The way Chuck worked, two years could stretch into four or five. That would give me plenty of time to finish another book. When the house was finally done, I could take a year off from writing to settle into it and start planning my log house in Door County. After Chuck and I bought the two acres on the ledge—splitting the cost as usual—I started reading up on llamas to prepare for the big changes we were planning, together and apart.

LLAMAS WERE BRED FROM GUANACO—the hump-less camels of the Andes—and were domesticated around 4,000 BC. The Incas used them mostly as pack animals. A 250-pound llama, standing 5 feet tall, could carry 100 pounds and travel 15 to 20 miles a day. The animals tolerated long periods of thirst at high altitudes, and their wool could be spun into yarn for clothes and rugs. Llamas were introduced to the United States at the beginning of the twentieth century as guard animals on sheep ranches. Their wool, sheared every two years, was brown, cream, white, or black.

The first time I saw llamas up close was at a "llama obstacle race" at a county fair in Milwaukee a few years back. The competing animals didn't "run" the course on their own; they were led through it, one at a time, by handlers who held their leash. The course started with a wooden gate from which hung plastic ribbons. Next came a long tippy board to walk on and a tub of water to wade through. Then the llama had to hop into and out of a horse trailer, walk over a rough patch of ground with branches strewn on it, and skip over a low stile to cross the finish line. Each llama had a particular obstacle he hated. The cream-colored one refused to walk through the gate, turning his head in distaste and backing out when the ribbons touched his cheek. The light brown animal balked before the tub of water, sat down, and had to be dragged across, and the black one insisted on walking around the stile instead of jumping over it, no matter how many times he was brought back in front of it. None of these animals went into the trailer without being pushed from behind. But the last llama, who was chocolate brown, breezed through the entire course two steps behind his handler, a portly man in a crisp white shirt, black jeans, and cowboy boots. People applauded and whistled when the pair crossed the finish line.

Later, I went over to the barn where the handlers were grooming their animals. I didn't see the champion llama or his handler, but an older woman in a jean jacket let me touch her cream-colored llama.

"He won't bite?" I asked

"Llamas only have one set of teeth so they can't bite. You can pet him on the neck."

When I put my hand on his neck, the llama sighed through his nose and made a humming sound.

"Hear that?" the woman said, "He's happy."

"He sounds like a cat," I said.

"Llamas and cats have their own minds. Working with them isn't like teaching tricks to dogs."

"I have a Siamese cat who lets me brush his teeth every night."

The woman laughed. "You might be good with llamas then," she said. She had a pleasant plain face and grey hair pulled back into a pony tail. In thirty years, I might look like an Asian version of her. I could retire from teaching and take up llama training as a hobby. When llamas decided they'd worked hard enough for the day or the load was too heavy—the race announcer had said—they knelt down on the trail and refused to budge. If threatened, they hissed and spat to show their displeasure. Passive but stubborn, they were animals I could identify with. Their wool, originally used by the common people (the smaller, softer alpacas were raised to provide wool for the nobility), was now spun into warm luxury yarns.

THE FIRST THING CHUCK WANTED to do to prepare our house for sale was to build an atrium.

"Our house is too small," he said. "An atrium would make it into the size more people would want. Dean says you always recoup your money from an atrium. Maybe he can build one for us." We didn't drive out to the schoolhouse anymore, but Dean occasionally came to town for errands and stopped for coffee. Though Katie hadn't signed the divorce papers he'd sent her, Jo and her daughter were already living in the schoolhouse.

Dean suggested a company near Madison that specialized in atriums. Chuck thought they would have models for us to walk around in, so we talked about making a weekend trip and stopping in Madison afterward. But before we could settle on a date, the first blizzard of the season dumped eight inches of snow in western Wisconsin.

"We should wait till spring," Chuck suggested. "Who wants to wander around the countryside looking at atriums in the snow? The place might be closed anyway."

"If it's too cold to visit these atriums in the winter," I asked, "do you think it's such a good idea to build one on our house?"

"I don't know," he shrugged. "It's a glass house. Maybe it comes with solar panels."

Our house had a gas furnace and forced-air vents. I hadn't thought about how the atrium would be heated. "There's a lot we haven't considered," I said.

"That's true," Chuck agreed. "I'll start renovating the upstairs. We'll talk about the atrium in the spring."

SO CHUCK STRIPPED THE WALLPAPER and scraped the paint from the spare room upstairs. Plaster crumbled in fist-sized pieces and scattered on the floor. We closed off the room so Dorian wouldn't lick the dust and get sick. "Maybe we need new drywall in there," Chuck said.

I wasn't sure what drywall was, but I asked, "Isn't that something we should hire a professional to do?"

"We'll take care of it later," Chuck answered. "I'll do the downstairs." He peeled off the wallpaper from the dining room, then the living room. To his relief the walls were plain white underneath, without the archeological layers of paint and wallpaper many people found in their renovation efforts. Maybe houses had their own karma and attracted the same kind of owners decade after decade. Whoever had built my basement writing room had put up two-by-fours to make a dropped ceiling but stopped halfway when they ran out of time or the materials. How hard was it to buy more two-by-fours, even I had wondered, but it never occurred to me to finish the job, either.

After taking down the wallpaper from the two rooms and scraping the paint off the back hallway, Chuck was tired of demolition. The hallway seemed like a good place to start re-painting, but when he brought back the color chart from the hardware store, we couldn't believe how many variations of white and off-white there were: atrium white, classic white, Navajo white, vanilla, wheat, parchment, ecru, cream, etc. In all the years of house painting, Chuck had never been asked to choose the color. For the exterior of our house, he'd used the leftover can he found in the basement and had it matched when he ran out.

"Maybe we could use a stain," he said. "Then we could leave the wood its natural color, more or less."

He planned to go back to the store for stain samples, but he must have known that they, too, would come in a dozen different colors and types and confuse him further. Weeks went by without either of us mentioning the back hallway. The weather began to change. When the annual Home and Garden show came to town, Chuck asked Dean to go with him so they could look into building the atrium. That company near Madison, or another one, would surely have a booth.

Chuck came home with a dozen clear plastic rolls that resembled the inflatable life-saving devices for children, the kind that wrapped around their arms.

"These are walls of water," he said, spreading them on the patio to demonstrate how each rib-like section could be filled with water. The walls then formed an insulating layer around the seedlings and the saplings.

"Dean got some for his trees," he explained, "and I thought we could use them, too, for the raspberry bushes in the back. I don't think an atrium is such a good idea for us after all. I should keep fixing the house without adding more to it. Next year when they have the Home and Garden show again, I should be ready to find a contractor and start planning the new house."

The atrium had shrunk into a dozen plastic tubes—see-through tents in which the raspberry bushes waited for better weather.

FOR THE NEXT YEAR AND A HALF, Chuck kept knocking the walls and tearing the floor. He didn't know how to build a new wall or lay down the tiles, but he was sure he could read up on the work when the time came. Periodically, I tried to remind him that we were supposed to make the house look better instead of worse. My talk was just like his repairs: I didn't know how to follow through. Chuck acted insulted whenever I suggested hiring a handyman or a carpenter to finish the job.

"I can do it myself," he said stiffly. "I just have to find the time."

"I'll hire someone to work as your assistant then. I know a lot of students who need summer jobs."

"That wouldn't help me. It's more trouble showing people how to do things."

Especially when you don't know how, I thought but didn't say.

"Do what you want, then," I told him instead. "It's up to you. I shouldn't be telling you how to do your job."

"No," Chuck said. "You shouldn't."

My writing room was yet untouched by Chuck's demolition, but it was only a matter of time before he got to the basement. When I heard that a colleague's husband, a photographer, was trying to rent out the upstairs of his portrait studio, I went to look.

The tiny apartment was divided into four cramped rooms: a kitchen that was more like a windowless hallway, a bathroom smaller than a utility closet, and two little rooms overlooking the one busy street in town. But when I shut the door behind me, I couldn't believe how peaceful the space felt. The photographer said I could bring my cat to work, so I signed the lease on the spot.

I hadn't consulted Chuck when I went to look at the studio, but he was thrilled when I told him I'd rented a place to write. Now he could play his stereo as loudly as he pleased while he tinkered around the house; he could even use the basement for his own storage. The move only took a few hours, with the help of the students I hired. My desk, loom, spinning wheel, and even the rabbits were now in my own space. The cat and I drove there every morning and returned to the house late at night. When I really needed to get away, I drove up to Door County and pitched my tent on my land or crashed on Norma Jean's couch.

I KNEW SO LITTLE ABOUT carpentry that I was planning to order a kit to build a summer home and another for a llama barn. Renovating the house was an enormous project with many complicated steps, and I had no idea where to begin, either. I had never been good at tackling a big job head-on. When I started a project or learned a new skill, I preferred to pin down a few simple details and figure out the rest by trial and error as I went along. That's why spinning and knitting came more easily to me than weaving.

Carpentry, like weaving, required precise, analytical thinking ahead of time: you couldn't take out a ceiling beam once the frame was in place; it was crazy to knock down the walls without a plan. Chuck was destroying our house by trying to renovate it the way I knitted a sweater: do a little of this, try a little of that, and see how things shape up. He should have evaluated the project first, broken it into manageable tasks, and finished them one at a time. Though I knew nothing about carpentry, I could have told him that much.

Thinking like a weaver was the most important skill I had learned from my hobbies, but weaving was a solitary activity. I did it alone at the loom, with the harnesses clattering and the shuttle swooshing. Even in a classroom with other weavers, there was no casual conversation. Although the craft had trained me in logical planning, it didn't prepare me to work with Chuck *and* make plans at the same time. Odysseus, the most famous protégée of Athene, the weaving goddess, was a terrible leader and a lousy partner. By the time he made it home, he had lost all his followers; in his absence, his wife had raised their son and defended their home by herself. He might have been a good-enough team player in the Trojan War, but he wasn't the leader of the Greek army; besides, compared to Achilles, everyone looked like an A+ team player. By nature, Odysseus was a lone hero.

Unlike the modern weaver, medieval tapestry weavers worked as a team, a dozen men standing side by side at the loom. The picture was divided into sections, and everyone was assigned his own narrow strip to weave. Their method was similar to intarsia knitting. The weft threads, kept on separate bobbins, stayed in the small areas where they were needed, instead of being carried all the way across the fabric; twisting them together at the color changes prevented holes. An average tapestry used twenty or more threads per inch. After a day's labor, a weaver finished an area the size of his hand, and his work lined up perfectly with the next weaver's. The weavers weren't collaborating with one another, however, in a fifty-fifty, give-and-take sense. The team followed the master plan (called a "cartoon") painted by the artist-designer of the tapestry. Their job was to carry out his vision, not to create their own picture together.

Chuck and I might have been able to renovate our house and build a new one if one of us had taken charge as the artist-designer, with the other following along like a team of weavers. But we only knew how to split everything down the middle, each of us meticulously sticking to our half—otherwise, one of us took on the entire task with no help from the other. With us, it was always 50-50 or 100-0. When Chuck told me that building a new house was going to be his project, he was quick to assure me that I wouldn't have to do a thing. Later, when it was clear he was struggling, I only offered to hire other people to help him. He might have been less insulted if I'd put myself forward as his assistant, if he could have done 80 % of the work with me picking up the remaining 20 % by running errands, preparing the surface he was painting, or cleaning up the debris he made.

I could also have taken charge of our need to move forward. "You should have a better plan," any normal person would have said to her husband. "Why not finish one thing at a time? Let me help you figure out what to do." But while our house got worse and worse, I just spent more time away from it. I couldn't make any suggestions to Chuck, because they were all variations of the one thing I had never asked anyone: *do this for me, if not for yourself*. If I had been able to say that at twelve, my mother wouldn't have killed herself.

AFTER CHUCK RIPPED out the floor boards and removed the doors from the cupboard, we could no longer cook in our kitchen. One night, as we were eating pizza off paper plates in the living room full of plaster dust, I imagined us living in one construction site or another for the next twenty years. This house or the new one in the country, it made no difference.

"Even if we built a house out in the country," I said, "I'm not sure if I want to move there with you."

"We don't have to live in the country," he responded. "We could sell that land and buy a bigger house in town. Maybe that wouldn't be a bad idea. I don't know if I'm ever going to be ready to build a new house."

I should have been relieved to hear him admit the truth for once, but all I felt was irritation. "But you were so enthusiastic about it before," I lashed out. "This whole thing was your idea to begin with."

"That's not true. You liked that two-acre lot more than I did."

"I never wanted to move out to the country. It's depressing to be stuck out in the middle of nowhere."

"That lot isn't out in the middle of nowhere," he said. "It's closer to your school than this house is."

We bickered about the location of the lot for the rest of the meal. Then while he was shoving the pizza box and the paper plates into the trash, I said, "Sometimes, I think I wouldn't mind living by myself again."

"You're kidding," Chuck laughed.

"No, I'm not," I said, but I remembered those nights Michiko packed the suitcase she had no intention of taking anywhere. I could almost hear her carrying on. "Okay," I conceded. "Maybe I'm just mad at you because you haven't finished the house in all this time."

"If you were so upset," he said, "you could have helped."

"I offered to hire someone, and you wouldn't even hear of it."

When we were exhausted from blaming each other for having to eat pizza off the floor, Chuck said, "We wouldn't be arguing like this if you were ready to leave."

"What would we be doing instead?" I asked.

"We'd be screaming at each other instead of bickering about food."

I was almost convinced he was right. Compared to other couples, I still thought, we got along well enough. But when friends asked me if I loved Chuck, I had no idea how to respond. I had never thought that my happiness depended on being with him or anyone. In the hours I spent alone at my desk or on the road, I felt completely at peace even if the writing or the running wasn't going particularly well. No one could give me the same satisfaction. Still, Chuck and I had been together for twelve years. All my grandparents and both my parents were dead, I didn't plan to see my brother ever again, and my remaining relatives were dwindling out of touch. Chuck was the only person I could think of as family. I wished he were my brother or cousin instead of my husband so we would always be related to each other. It took me another year to figure out that this wasn't a good reason for us to stay married.

With Hiroshi gone, I didn't need to be *related* to anyone. During his life, in spite of the distance I'd put between us, a letter from him could make me question everything I cared about. In his eyes, I was always less than nothing. I had wanted Chuck to be my family as an alternative to the father who continued to undermine me no matter what I chose to do. From the beginning, our marriage was meant to keep me from returning to Hiroshi's house in defeat. But now, if I decided to live alone, my father wasn't around to call me selfish or ridicule me for failing to stay married. His death meant I finally had only one home, the place where I chose to live, not that other place I was afraid of being dragged back to. When Chuck started tearing the wallpaper from our bedroom walls, I moved out to my studio.

Chuck and I used to think of ourselves as free spirits afraid of nothing, but in truth, we were terrified of change. When we married, we told ourselves that we had already made a commitment by moving in together so marriage was an afterthought. We bought the first house we saw and the first piece of land we found outside a subdivision: they were "meant to be" ours. We could only accept a big change after the fact, when all the important decisions had been made by fate or by ourselves with so little awareness that it might as well have been fate. By the time we separated, I had my own apartment and five acres of land where I intended to build a summer home. My pets were used to spending time in my studio and, when I opened the tiny closet in one of the two cramped rooms, I was surprised to see that most of my clothes were already there. After Chuck tore out the shower from our house, I had been running from my studio. While he was demolishing our house, I had moved my possessions—a handful at a time—to my new home.

Our whole marriage had been the opposite of a marriage. We had been so careful, from the beginning, not to make any promises about the future. We kept separate bank accounts, cars, friends, weekend plans. In the thirteen years we lived together, we hadn't gotten any closer to having one shared life. We were like Penelope, who wove her tapestry during the day and unraveled it at night so that every morning, she was facing the same picture as the day before. But unweaving was hard work. With a knitted fabric, all you have to do is snip one stitch and pull the yarn. To unweave, you have to treadle the loom, following the pattern exactly backward, and unpack the threads that have been packed together. Wool, which has "memory," sticks together and has to be tugged apart. I was surprised by how hard it was to leave even when I knew I was doing the right thing.

In the first few months after I moved out, Chuck and I had many tearful conversations about how we might still "change the way we do things" and stay together. After every conversation, I left confused, only to be relieved and clear-headed as soon as I was alone in my car driving back to my studio. I didn't want to live with Chuck no matter how he changed, or with anyone else. I loved being alone. Once I knew that, it was pointless to talk about our future together. I never found out why Chuck took to un-building our old house instead of building a new one. He said he planned to finish the house someday and relocate to the countryside by himself.

I FILLED OUT THE DIVORCE papers at the same *pro se* office Dean had used. Unlike Katie, who took two years to sign their papers, Chuck didn't stall or try to change my mind. I had been living in my apartment for a year by the time we were filing the papers, and he had been renovating the house for three. He had painted some of the walls and hired workmen to put in the floors and fix the shower, but the bedrooms had no wallpaper. When he was done with the renovation, he said, he would move much farther out of town than the two of us had planned to. I didn't want him to sell the house prematurely, so we agreed on half the equity I had accumulated and signed a contract saying he would pay me that amount whenever he was able to in the next twenty-five years. Because Chuck needed funds to complete the repairs and I had some money saved, I bought out his share of the land on the ledge and kept it along with my Door County land. We talked about how ironic it was I'd ended up with that lot. Although I continued to camp on my land in Door County, I never again went to look at those two acres where I once imagined living with Chuck and the llamas. A part of me couldn't believe we were never going to be an old farm couple hearing the great grey owls hooting in the trees.

At our divorce hearing, we asked the judge if we could sit together instead of occupying the separate tables set out for us. We sat side by side holding hands, something we seldom did in public. More than ever, we resembled two panels in an intarsia pattern, contrasting colors lightly twisted at the edge. We thought we could go on being separate but together for the rest of our lives, even after the judge pronounced our marriage "irrevocably broken."

Cardigans

THE ONLY WAY TO DESIGN a cardigan as three tubes knitted together is to make a pullover and cut it open down the middle. "Cut on basting, then lie down in a darkened room for fifteen minutes to recover," Elizabeth Zimmermann advised in *Knitting Without Tears*. "You will never fear to cut again. (But always be sure to cut at the right place.)" Since I couldn't be so sure, I never made cardigans in my first twelve years of knitting. They were too fussy and feminine, I decided—favorites of 1950s cheerleaders and suburban housewives.

Actually, the cardigan started out as a military uniform in England in the nineteenth century. James Thomas Brudenell, 7th Earl of Cardigan, spent his own money to keep his cavalry regiment looking smart, and the knitted waistcoat he introduced became known as "the cardigan jacket." The earl was legendary for his bad temper rather than for his sartorial excellence. He wounded one of his own officers in a duel, illegally placed another under arrest, and was stripped of his command for his undue severity, but his family's influence secured him another post. In 1854, at age fifty-seven, he went to fight in the Crimean War as major general.

His cavalry was stationed on the heights above Balaklava, a British supply port on the Black Sea. When an order came for them to march down into a valley guarded by the Russians, the earl sent back a query to make sure. His superior repeated the order, so Cardigan led his men into the valley where the Russian cannons, muskets, and rifles fired at them from every side. 40% of the soldiers died. Tennyson wrote "The Charge of the Light Brigade" to celebrate their bravery. Cardigan was lionized on his return to England and appointed inspector general of cavalry. When another military man published a book falsely asserting that Cardigan had not led the famous charge, the earl sued him for libel. Cardigan died at seventy by falling off a horse in peace time. Like my father, he was a volatile and arrogant man obsessed with his reputation. The Battle of Balaklava had been indecisive at best, and the famous charge had made no difference in the outcome.

In the twentieth century, the gallant military jacket became the button-down sweater worn mostly by women. Mr. Rogers and Perry Como, the two cardigan-clad men of my father's generation, came from small towns in Pennsylvania. Fred Rogers was a puppeteer and a Presbyterian minister before he made his debut as Mr. Rogers. Perry Como started sweeping up in a barber shop when he was ten years old and sang as he worked. His mellow baritone voice and easy-going manner eventually made him a popular TV host, but the movies he starred in were considered unremarkable. His personality wasn't flashy enough for Hollywood. He and Mr. Rogers occupied the opposite end of the spectrum from the Earl of Cardigan.

My friends in Green Bay and Door County, too, were nice guys from small towns. Some even wore the old-fashioned camel-colored cardigans with wooden buttons. The more stylish, like Jim the priest, preferred the wholesome J. Crew look, which was an updated version of the same thing. Pete, the librarian who fell asleep at the movies, wrote and directed children's puppet shows. Don was a minister; Jeff volunteered as a reading coach and a Big Brother. The others worked as high school counselors, college professors, graphic designers, or restaurant managers. They were steady, low-key people. If they took on an ambitious job like remodeling their house, they set a realistic goal and met it in a reasonable amount of time. They didn't get obsessed with their project or paralyzed by it. I loved my friends, but I wasn't attracted to them.

Chuck hated Mr. Rogers' naive and cheerful manner. Though he, too, was low-key, he was far from steady or mild-mannered. He refused to make his students recite the Pledge of Allegiance; he had them listen to Jimi Hendrix's rendition of the National Anthem instead. He scorned fellow teachers who were afraid to utter "the f-word" even when no students or parents were around to hear them. His motto behind the wheel was "when in doubt, drive offensively." Chuck was the biggest, most unapologetic under-achiever I knew. All the great funny stories he told me on the night we met were about how little he'd accomplished by any conventional standard in the ten years since high school graduation. The joy he took in not settling down was what I loved about him and why I couldn't be with him anymore.

THE INTARSIA SWEATER DESIGNED by Norma Jean, my Door County neighbor, had a boat neck, dropped shoulders, and dolman sleeves. The first sweater I ever knitted from a pattern, in four flat pieces instead of three tubes, it looked more feminine than any garment I owned. For years, I had worn the same pullovers and T-shirts with baggy jeans or sweat pants. Almost forty, I still dressed like a boy in junior high school. Looking sloppy was my version of being an under-achiever, of endlessly demolishing the house instead of renovating it.

I was drawn to the mohair shrugs and lacy merino cardigans displayed at yarn stores, and yet I only made unisex pullovers. Some had bright colors, elaborate cable panels, or Fair Isle patterns, but all were shapeless. The few accessories I'd designed for myself, like the angora-fox, were quirky and whimsical instead of gorgeous. I only made beautiful things for friends—hats trimmed with silk roses, scarves with long braided fringes, evening bags embellished with beads. I had made little progress since choosing that yellow yarn for the first-ever knitting project in the seventh grade. My mother's death had separated me from beauty.

WHENEVER TAKAKO PLANNED A NEW dress for me, the two of us used to look through the pattern books and go to the fabric store together. The salesladies unrolled bolts of cotton, wool, or velvet and opened drawer after drawer of buttons, some sewn onto cards, others loose inside white enameled boxes. Finding the right fabric, notions, and embellishment was a treasure hunt. During the weeks my mother spent cutting the cloth, basting, sewing, and embroidering, she had me try on the dress several times to make sure I liked the way it was turning out. My mother's taste for me was very feminine. She preferred puffed sleeves, frills at the hem, flowers embroidered onto the bodice, a bow in the back, a lace collar. These dresses were entirely different from my classmates' store-bought shirts, skirts, and shorts. My clothes resembled what my mother wore in her more elegant, adult way.

Back then, it never occurred to me that women dressed to please men. My father was seldom around, so my mother spent her weekends and evenings with my brother and me. During the day when we were at school, she was alone at home or having tea with the women in our building. When she came to our school plays and concerts, she saw other mothers and our teachers, most of whom were women. Takako kept a courteous distance from the storekeepers and workmen she did business with; she had never met the fathers of my school friends, and she only knew her neighbors' husbands well enough to say hello to if they passed each other on the street. The only men she talked to regularly were her father and brothers. My friends' mothers, my aunts, our women neighbors all said that my mother was beautiful. When my grandfather and uncles praised her, they said she was smarter than anyone they knew. I could only conclude that men didn't notice what women wore or looked like.

⤸

DURING THE FIRST MONTH my stepmother lived at our house, I woke up in the middle of the night and went downstairs to get a snack. The light was on in the kitchen, but I scarcely noticed. By the time I stopped, I was standing between the hallway and the kitchen, and Michiko was glaring at me from the table where she was seated, pouring whiskey into a glass. Her pink nightgown, made of nylon, was sheer and low cut. My father, whose back was toward me, had on his boxer shorts but no shirt. As she handed the glass to him, Michiko raised her chin and pointed at me with her face.

Hiroshi turned around. "What are you doing?" he asked. "Why aren't you sleeping?"

I could have asked him the same thing, but I didn't. I ran back to my room without answering. Although I wouldn't find out the "facts of life" for six more months, I started noticing how tight Michiko's pants were. She wore clingy shirts that she didn't button all the way to the top. Even when she wasn't in her nightgown, she was trying to get my father to see through her clothes. Once, after she got a haircut she liked, she said her hair looked so good, because her new hair stylist was a man. "Only a man can really see how a woman looks," she gushed. I didn't think her hair looked particularly good then or ever, but her comment made me uneasy. She was saying that her hair stylist and my father both had special see-through vision because they were men.

When she got rid of the dresses my mother had made for me, Michiko said I was too old to be wearing frilly dresses with bows and embroidery. The pant suits she put in my closet were too big. No real mother would buy clothes for their daughter without the two of them going shopping together to try them on. I threw them out as soon as I started buying my own clothes at fifteen. Like my friends, I wore jeans, T-shirts, sweaters. For the first and last time in my life, I blended into the crowd. But when we turned eighteen, my friends went shopping with their mothers for their new wardrobe of tailored dresses, loose-fitting blouses, and long skirts—tasteful clothes that advertised their modesty as much as Michiko's outfits flaunted her lack of it. Either way, I saw, women dressed to attract men, to send them a message. Although that was true enough, men had nothing to do with why I went out of my way to emphasize my plainness. I envied my friends' shopping trips with their mothers, the long afternoons they spent at the beauty salon getting haircuts and manicures together. After all these years, I was still stuck in the same limbo of a motherless teenager. I felt sorry for myself for having no one to fuss over me.

THE SECOND SWEATER I MADE from a pattern came from a book published by Rowan, a British yarn company. The dozen sweaters in it all had names—Kiri, Steffi, Miss Brown, Miriam—or maybe the names referred to the models. "Miriam" sat on a blue bench in front of a blue house leaning against a grey-haired man, the blue of her cable cardigan matching the background color of his Fair Isle pullover. At the bottom of the picture, barely visible in tiny letters like subtitles of a French movie, the direction said, "Miriam in DK Tweed by Debbie Bliss, pattern page 85." I flipped through the book and found the sweater diagramed with precise measurements, yarn recommendations, gauge requirements, and step-by-step directions you had to be fully awake—not leaning so languidly against a man old enough to be your father—to understand. It was like meeting the same person twice and being impressed by how really smart she was.

I chose Emmeline, another cardigan, because its peplum waist had tiny twisted cables like the embellishment on my mother's heathered pullover. The recommended yarn, a mixture of mohair and lambswool, made a fuzzy halo like that pullover, but the cardigan had a boxier, padded-shouldered look. Emmeline in the book's photograph was brown, worn by an Irish beauty with raven-black hair and icy blue eyes, but the yarn came in a dozen other colors.

I chose dark green, the color of the tea Takako and I had sipped in a temple garden in Kyoto on a spring afternoon when I was ten. The tiny pink cake served with the tea was sweeter than anything I'd ever tasted because its purpose, my mother explained, was to deepen the rich bitterness of the tea. If it hadn't been for the astonishing contrast between those two tastes, I might not have remembered that afternoon so clearly: the cherry blossoms and the rocks of the temple garden, the sun falling on the straw mats of the tea room, my mother and me lifting the heavy cups to our lips. Bitter and sweet always went together. If my father or stepmother had loved me, if I had been happy with them, I might have forgotten Takako as my brother had. Because I was a girl, I had gotten to spend time alone with Takako even after he was born.

Once I stitched the knitted pieces together and sewed on the pearl buttons from an old fabric store whose dusty drawers contained threads and button cards from decades ago, the green cardigan resembled the nettle shirts in my mother's bedtime story. Takako hadn't read that story only to keep up her own courage in my father's absence. Long before she became unhappy enough to kill herself, she must have had a premonition. Surely, she meant to warn me about the future. She might have been disappointed. I had turned out to be nothing like the brave knitting princess who triumphed over the two evil queens— the witch and the mother-in-law. I had more in common with the brothers who flew away.

Afraid to soar higher or to come down to the ground, the swan-boy kept beating his awkward wings. He had nothing to hold on to in that thin air above the tree tops, and yet he was stuck. The sky refused to release him.

That was my story so far, but the beauty my mother had shown me hadn't disappeared. In a story retold night after night, as in a dream, I could be anyone—even two people at once. I was both the sister and the brother, the one releasing the magic shirt she'd labored over for so long, and the other landing at her feet, finally, to accept it. To break the spell, I had to stop the endless circling.

FIVE

Flip-Flop Mittens

T HE THREE GODDESSES OF FATE in Greek myth were spinners. In a small room behind the kitchen in the palace of the gods, the first treadled the wheel, the second measured the thread, and the third lopped it off. They were older than all the others on Mount Olympus, and even Zeus was afraid of them. When a race of giants attacked the palace, the fates chased them away with a golden pestle from the kitchen. No one could fight against them and win. The thread they made determined each mortal's life span.

My grandmother, Fuku, and her two sisters, Masu and Ko, seemed as mysterious to me as the fates. At a family reunion in Kobe in the early 1960s, they were seated side by side at the head table, each wearing a grey kimono, her white hair put up in a bun. When I went to greet them and said, "Obahchan"—Grandmother—they turned to me at once, their faces wrinkled into identical smiles. Their bent backs and short necks, each with a hump at the base, looked exactly the same. It was as though my grandmother had split herself into three people.

The women were barely in their sixties then. They had grown up in a prosperous home in Himeji, a castle town, and their names read together, "Masu Kofuku," meant "increasing happiness." After the war, when all three lost their land, my grandmother became convinced that they had been punished for their parents' arrogance in choosing such auspicious names. To prevent more bad luck from befalling our family, she suggested the humblest of names for her two oldest grandchildren. Mine, Kyoko, meant "respectful" and my brother's, Jumpei, "mild-mannered and humble." Our two names together, "Kyo-jun," meant "absolute and humble obedience." By the time we were born, the bombed-out buildings in our city had been replaced by high-rises. Other children had optimistic names: Machiko ("polishes her intellect"), Kazumi ("harmonious and beautiful"), Susumu ("marching forward"), Makoto ("absolute truth"), Tadashi ("justice and integrity"), Ryukichi ("lucky dragon boy").

The women in my grandmother's family were famous for their longevity. Widowed in their seventies, Masu, Ko, and Fuku would each manage alone instead of becoming a burden to her children; all three would die in their nineties from heart failure or pneumonia. The moral of their story was that you shouldn't wish for too much. The greatest virtue was in being content with less.

THE FEW PIECES OF FURNITURE I bought for my studio were cheap and light-weight, intended for students, widowers, divorcees, and other people in transition, but I was going nowhere. I had the same teaching job, volunteer activities, and weekly get-togethers with friends in Green Bay and Door County. I shopped at the grocery stores whose layout I could describe in my sleep and ran and biked the routes I had figured out years before. Dorian lived with me but stayed with Chuck when I traveled out of town, so even his routine was undisturbed.

The only other time I had faced a major change—moving from Kobe to Rockford—I had attended classes and studied in the library as before, listened to the music I already knew, and worn the clothes I'd bought in Kobe. I had arranged my dorm room to look just like my room at Hiroshi's house, with the bed and the desk against one wall, the dresser against the other, and the Indian "Tree of Life" tapestry from a junior high school bazaar tacked on the ceiling. A similar tapestry now covered my futon bed. I hadn't experienced any real change since my mother's death, because I had become an expert at keeping everything the same.

When I first moved into my studio, I had considered building my log house in Door County right away or buying a condo in Milwaukee and commuting to my teaching job. By the time the divorce was final, the thought of all that driving back and forth, week after week, exhausted me. I didn't even have the energy to find a larger apartment in town.

Chuck and I played tennis once a week—hitting the ball back and forth without keeping score—and ate dinner at the restaurants we'd gone to a hundred times. The only change was that I had him over for coffee in my studio, a space I had never shared with him during our marriage. One night as he was leaving, he told me how upset he was with his mother for being so critical of him; another night, he said he was worried about a childhood friend who was drinking himself to death. When I complained about my job, he shook his head and said, "That's terrible. No wonder you're upset. You deserve better." My college was becoming more like a business school every year. I dreaded staying there till retirement, but I was afraid to give up a secure job I already knew how to do. "I feel the same way about my job," he admitted. "It's scary to stay or to leave."

I used to have dreams in which my mother came to visit me. We had deeply satisfying conversations I couldn't remember on waking, except that all the time we were talking we both knew she was dead. Chuck and I seemed to be floating through our afterlife within this lifetime. Just like in my dreams, a part of me always knew that we were only having our great conversations, because our real life was already over. I didn't wish we hadn't split up. I only wanted to stay in this afterlife with him forever.

In October and November, as the days grew shorter, we found a deserted tennis court on the edge of town. Maybe the city forgot to turn off the lights in that park. Long after the other courts had closed, the single court by the river was illuminated at night. By four o'clock, when Chuck met me in the empty parking lot, dusk was falling. The last flocks of geese flew overhead, wave after wave of black shadows. We played wearing our hats and gloves, and the ball bounced differently now that the asphalt was so cold. In Milwaukee, near our apartment, a small group of old men had played tennis year round on the lakeside court the city had plowed especially for them. For all our talk of living for now and not planning for the future, we'd envisioned ourselves being like them someday: two stubborn people defying winter and old age, united in our eccentricity and rebellion. But when our riverside court got buried in snow in December, the city didn't send out a plow to clear it for us. Chuck and I talked about joining the indoor tennis club that had just opened in town, but neither of us took the initiative.

WHEN I WENT TO JAPAN on my sabbatical trip, I was planning to start a novel about my family's experiences during World War II. I came back with pages of journal entries from my conversations with Fuku. No matter how many times I went over them, I couldn't piece together a novel. I couldn't even manage a biographical account of Fuku's struggles as a mother of six in the 1940s.

I didn't know my grandmother well enough to tell her story, real or imagined, that didn't include me. I had returned to Japan hoping to understand my family as an adult, only to realize that I had become a stranger to them. Except in journals and in school compositions about how I'd spent my summer vacation, I had never written directly about myself, but this story of my trip was about me instead of Fuku, and it could only be told as a memoir.

If I could write the way I cooked or knitted—recreating the same pasta dishes and pullover sweaters with only minor variations—I would have. As much as other people yearned for adventure, I craved stability. The pleasure of following the same recipe or pattern was in noticing the special tang of basil from the garden in late summer or the particular delicacy of lace knitted in the palest shade of pink. I loved those quiet moments when things were almost but not exactly the same. But in writing, the best passages came to me either as a complete surprise—whole sentences effortlessly appearing in the back of my mind—or else they were the result of so many agonized revisions that, later, I couldn't bear to recall how I'd arrived at the final version. Either way, the not-knowing was the price I had to pay to write the few sentences among many that gave me the most pleasure. Once I got something right, I couldn't do it again.

After several false starts with the memoir, I began to see how my recent trip was a journey into the long-ago past. Unlike the novel, the memoir made me reflect directly on the events I had glossed over in my mind while I was experiencing them. Instead of moving sideways in a fictional maneuver to examine a situation *like* the one that had confused and pained me, I now had a chance to re-experience that same situation as time stopped on the page. In the quiet of my studio, under pressure from no one but myself, I could put aside the pretense and the self-delusion and finally examine my own true thoughts and feelings.

But understanding the past didn't boost my courage to face the future. Every month when I leafed through the national job list from the writers' organization, I decided my job wasn't so bad and Green Bay was all right. When Chuck and I couldn't repair our house, I'd assumed that our passivity was his fault or the pitfall of having to make a joint decision as a couple. As it turned out, I could immobilize myself all on my own. When my writing was going well, I was terrified of jinxing the good streak by attempting even the smallest change in my daily routine; when I hit a snag, I was too preoccupied to think of anything else.

Two summers after our divorce, Dorian died at eighteen, so I no longer stopped at the house on my way in and out of town to drop him off or pick him up. If I came to visit, I called ahead and knocked on the door like any other guest. The cat had been the keeper of our marriage's afterlife. Although Chuck and I still played tennis and went to dinner, I understood it wouldn't be forever. I didn't know what was on the other side of that change, and I didn't want to find out.

WHAT MOBILIZED ME AT LAST was a series of coincidences I could attribute to fate. I finished my memoir and Michael Collier, the new director of the Bread Loaf Writers' Conference, happened to read it on a plane. When he telephoned and offered me a fellowship I hadn't applied for, I accepted in surprise.

I had long admired the established writers who were on the faculty that summer, but during the two-week conference, I was too shy to approach them. Most of the other fellows—new writers with one or two books—were from New York or Boston. I ate my meals and took walks with the few others who were from small towns. On the last day, two writers from Cambridge were comparing their favorite places to walk with their daughters and promising to get together. I didn't know anyone in town, besides Jim, who understood what I did from day to day. When I returned to Green Bay, I couldn't help feeling that something was lacking.

So when one of the writers from Bread Loaf recommended me for a summer teaching job at the Loft in Minneapolis, I was eager to go. The people at the Loft introduced me to the local writers. In the classes I taught, the students were full-grown adults and very motivated. What I liked the best, though, was that no one looked at me as I ran or walked around the Uptown neighborhood where my apartment was. I couldn't believe how comfortable it was to be left alone for thirty-one days straight—never stared at or asked to respond to a mangled greeting in Japanese. If I lived in a city, I could just *be*.

In early August of 1998, when another job list came in the mail, I had just gotten back to Green Bay from Minneapolis. As I read the ad for a five-year lectureship at Harvard to teach nonfiction writing, I remembered the two writers at Bread Loaf discussing their morning strolls around a reservoir. I typed my curriculum vitae, wrote a letter of application, and sent them off. A month later, when the department secretary called and said I should forward my dossier and send my books, I assumed they asked everyone who had applied.

I had attended schools no one had heard of and taught at one that was even more obscure. The only awards I'd ever received were from regional organizations like the Wisconsin Library Association. My dossier had letters from my current colleagues and former teachers in Milwaukee and Rockford. After forwarding it in early September, I heard nothing more about the job. Most schools waited until they made their final choice, then sent out mass mail announcing the result. In the meantime, no news usually meant you were already eliminated.

By the first week of December, if I'd thought about the job at all, it was to wonder where the mass mail was and if I'd remembered to enclose an envelope to get my books back. The message I found on my answering machine one night, asking me to come to Cambridge for an on-campus interview, shocked me. The next morning, when the secretary faxed me the names of the people who would be interviewing me, I realized why I hadn't gotten eliminated. One of the writers on the search committee had been on the faculty at Bread Loaf the year I was a fellow, so she must have recognized my name and put my application in the pile for further consideration.

There were four five-year lectureships like the one I was applying for, and Henri Cole—a poet I knew from graduate school—was finishing his. I hadn't wanted to embarrass him by asking about my application. Now that I was coming to town for an interview, though, I thought maybe I should call him. Two days before I left, I finally got around to it.

"I heard you were on the list," he said right away. "I'm not a part of this search, but they really like you."

"I didn't call till now because I didn't want to bother you," I said. "I don't expect you to help me."

"You don't need my help," he said.

"It's no big deal. I never expected to get this far. There must be a dozen other people who are better qualified."

"Not anymore. You're one of the three they're still considering."

I was too stunned to speak. The interview was scheduled for only one hour. I wasn't being asked to teach a class or meet with anyone besides the committee, so I'd assumed this wasn't yet the final round.

"It's been a good job for me," Henri continued. "The students are great, and I've had a lot of time to write. If they offered you the job, would you take it?"

"If they made an offer," I said, "it would be like having a magic wand waved over me to change my life completely."

"I hope you get your wish then," Henri said. For the first time since I sent the application, I imagined myself living in a real city and teaching at an Ivy-league school. My apartment felt more cramped and shabby than ever. I had outgrown the modest life I'd made in Green Bay. But it was preposterous to wish for a teaching job at a college I wouldn't have gotten into as a student. Like a foolish character from the Brothers Grimm, I wished I could take back my wish.

IN HIGH SCHOOL, I'd performed so poorly under pressure that my teachers started excusing me from tests and giving me take-home exams. Otherwise, I got nosebleed or migraine headaches, went to the nurse's office, and fell into deep coma-like sleep I never experienced otherwise. In sports, in the final set of a close volleyball game, I lobbed an underhand serve I could get over the net with everyone watching instead of the killer roundhouse serve I had practiced for hours every week. Even as an adult, I could only win a 10K race by going out so fast that I didn't have to see my competition after the first mile. If anyone was close enough to make a move in the last mile, I backed off and let her pass—no big deal, I told myself, the other runner cared more about winning

I didn't ask Henri who the other two candidates were, because if I knew their names I wouldn't be able to get on the plane. The only way I could go to a job interview at Harvard was to pretend it was a practice run for the more likely jobs I might apply for in the future. Still, with only two days remaining, it occurred to me to find out more about the people who would be interviewing me. Even my college's library had their books, so I checked them out to read on the plane. An hour before the interview, I was still skimming through the last one, but the hotel was directly across the street from the interview.

When I walked into the room, I was glad to have read the books. As I shook hands with the people on the committee, I felt less stupid for knowing their work. Surprisingly, I had an answer for every question they asked about my writing and teaching. At the end, the woman who had been at Bread Loaf hugged me instead of shaking my hand. The afternoon we'd met in Middlebury, in front of one of the houses on campus, a bird had flown into a window and fallen on the grass at her feet and she had screamed. That was the only time we actually talked. She must have been impressed to see me pick up that bird and take him back to my room. Most birds that hit their heads either fly away immediately or die in a few days. That bird—an Eastern bluebird—was no exception to the latter, but like a creature from the fairy tales, he had repaid me by making the woman remember me.

"You'll get the job," Henri said when I met him for dinner.

I laughed and shook my head.

"I'm staying in town next year to teach at Brandeis," he added. "It would be nice to be neighbors again."

The last time we'd lived in the same city, I had inherited his apartment and his furniture when he finished his master's and moved to New York. The red couch Chuck and I sat on when we decided to move to Green Bay together used to belong to Henri. I wasn't sure if that was a good or a bad omen.

"You can have my office this time," Henri offered.

The next day when I got home, the light was blinking on my answering machine. I walked in and played the message, already knowing what it was and not believing it at the same time. The chair of the search committee had left her home number so I could call as soon as possible to accept.

My superiors didn't try to talk me into staying or offer me a leave of absence so I could come back. I had taught my last fall semester in Green Bay without knowing it. My friends said how much they would miss me, but they had been prepared for my departure. "I didn't think you were going to stay here," even Chuck said. I wrote my letter of resignation and delivered it in a daze. The biggest change in my adult felt more like an act of the fates than a move I had chosen and planned for myself—until I started looking for a new home.

THE SEARCH COMMITTEE AT HARVARD, who didn't seem worried in the least about my giving up a tenured job for a temporary one, had emphasized how difficult it was going to be for me to find an apartment in Cambridge. The week before Christmas, I contacted the three lecturers Henri taught with and asked them where they lived and how much rent or mortgage they paid. I was quizzing strangers over the phone about their finances and living arrangements—during the holiday season, no less—but everyone was eager to tell their story. The woman I'd be replacing was a single mother with a small rental apartment far from campus; she was building a house in Alaska for the summers and didn't care where she lived the rest of the year. "You should try Somerville," she said, "where people are more working-class and less snooty." If I preferred small, working-class towns, I would stay in Green Bay. The next person I talked to, one of the fiction writers, rented an old house on a beach in Cape Cod, two hours away, and slept in his office on the days he taught. He, too, said it was impossible to find anything near Harvard. The other fiction writer, the last to get back to me, told a different story. She had managed to buy a condo near campus even though, at the time, she had a terrible credit record and she was being audited by the IRS. I asked her to put me in touch with her realtor, whose name was Pebble.

Henri lived in a condo in Boston, in a gentrified neighborhood that had once been "marginal." He, too, thought I should buy rather than rent. After examining the weekly property listings Pebble faxed me, I flew to Cambridge, where it only took a few hours to see all the nine listings in my price range. The first was a studio on the top floor of a four-story brownstone a mile from campus. It was divided into three separate spaces beside the bathroom: a living room, an alcove (a very small bedroom without a closet), and a galley kitchen. The large windows faced the east and overlooked the tops of maple trees. The neighborhood reminded me of Milwaukee's East Side, with a mix of single houses and brownstones, a grocery store and a cafe around the corner. The other eight listings were lofts and efficiencies with the kitchen appliances crammed into the corner of the one big room. I marked their locations on the map Henri had given me, collected the realtors' brochures, and took notes, but I couldn't see living in any of these. Some had high ceilings and others had nice woodwork; one was on the river but the view wasn't enough. Even my shabby apartment in Green Bay had more than one room.

I asked Pebble to take me back to the first place. This time, I noticed the pansies planted along the walkway to the beveled-glass door of the building, the polished woodwork on the stairway, and inside the tiny apartment, the hardwood floors and the built-in book case. The galley kitchen had roomy cabinets, a peg board, and enough counter space for baking bread or assembling a casserole. While the other listings were in old Victorian houses and small factory buildings that had been cut up into apartments in the 1960s, the studio was in a brownstone—built in the 1920s—that had thirty apartments of various sizes. The space I was standing in was always meant to be exactly what it was: a single person's home.

Still, I didn't make an offer right away, as Chuck and I had done in Green Bay. I waited a day and asked to see the apartment one more time with Henri. We even went back to the few others that had a good view or a nice closet, but that first apartment really was the only one I could see living in. There was no reason, then, to keep looking or to quibble over a few thousand dollars with the seller, who insisted on the full listing price. By the time I flew back to Green Bay, I'd met with the mortgage broker, walked through the apartment with a building inspector, and gotten the mortgage application approved and the purchase agreement signed. I called a moving company and set the date for mid-May so I could spend my summer settling in my new home instead of saying good-bye.

TO RAISE MY DOWN PAYMENT, I had sold the land on the ledge where Chuck and I once planned to build a house. I was getting ready to sell my Door County land, too, when Chuck told me he would refinance the house and give me the equity he owed me from our divorce. "Then you can keep your Door County land and still find a place to live out east. I'm planning to visit your summer house someday."

Instead of waiting or thinking about it or wondering where to go, he called his credit union right away and got the money. If I had sold my Door County land anyway and added the proceeds to the down payment, I could have bought a one-bedroom apartment instead of a tiny studio. But my job in Cambridge was temporary. I had no interest in relocating permanently to the east coast. When my lectureship was over, I would find a tenured job in Chicago or Minneapolis and build my log house in Door County. Then I could have a big city life in the Midwest and a retreat in Door County, with the friends I'd already made. For the first time as an adult, I felt decisive and competent: I had a long-range plan instead of staying where I was by default.

A FEW DAYS BEFORE I LEFT, Chuck and his parents took me out to dinner to celebrate. His mother told me I should stay in touch and be sure to visit, and his father said he was proud of me. After they went home, Chuck and I drank coffee in my studio amid the moving boxes, talking till midnight about nothing important. When the time came for him to leave, he said, "I'll come and visit you out east, so let's not say good-bye."

I walked him down the steps, we hugged, and then he drove away. On the cross-country move in my car, the first leg was the reverse of the journey the two of us and Dorian had taken with our boxes and plants when we'd moved to Green Bay. I was traveling backwards, alone. In Milwaukee, I stopped for coffee in our old neighborhood, and in Kenosha, at the Amoco station near where his sister Chris had lived for a year when her children were very young. I was in Ohio the next day, where the interstate was called "the turnpike," before I knew, for certain, that I had left our old life and was on my own now.

BEFORE THE MOVERS ARRIVED, I had to decide where everything should go. I had taken pictures of my furniture on special "Write-On" Polaroid film and recorded the dimensions. I now measured the walls and the floors of my empty apartment, diagrammed the layout, taped the furniture photographs on the walls, and marked the floor with masking tape. I measured, calculated, and re-measured as if I were planning a big weaving project. If all the furniture fit just right, the alcove could be my writing room, with the bigger room serving as a dining room, living room, and bedroom in one. In my sleeping bag, placed exactly where the bed would go, I felt the slant of the hardwood floor against my spine and remembered the nights I'd spent camping on my land. More than a thousand miles away, I was cutting back the invisible junipers and carving my paths around the new home.

After the furniture was in place, my first guest was Henri. We ate the jar of pesto I'd made in Green Bay and the bread I baked from the sour dough starter transported across several state lines in my cooler. In my new living/dining room, we sat on the kitchen chairs he had given me twenty years before in Milwaukee, so the meal was a communion with all the places of my past. The first house guest arrived before the week was out. One of the guys in my movie group from Green Bay had gotten laid off from his job and decided to take a road trip. I gave up my bed to him and slept on the floor of my new writing room. My head tucked under the desk and my legs scrunched against the radiator, I could see a tiny piece of the sky framed in the corner of the window. It was oddly like sitting in the backseat of my own car and getting a tilted view of a familiar road. Eager to show him the sights, I learned how to get around the city. I had stumbled on to the one thing that had been lacking in my studio in Green Bay. Entertaining turned a single person's apartment into a home.

The very layout of my new apartment expressed what home meant to me: a large room I could share with guests, a small room where I could be alone to write, a kitchen where I could cook a single meal or a big dinner. Living alone made me appreciate the company I chose, but I wasn't a person who moved easily from a day of writing to an evening of conversations. I liked gradual transitions, borders and boundaries, nooks and crannies, with plenty of blank spaces in between. Even in a place I had to myself, I preferred to keep things separate—solitude and company, writing and living, cooking and knitting. But equally important was the fact that I wanted all of these activities under the same roof to make a home.

IN GREEN BAY, DOOR COUNTY, and Minneapolis, once I got to know someone, I met a dozen of their friends who welcomed me into their circle. Our get-togethers were casual and impromptu, often involving food. Those who enjoyed cooking might call the rest of us and ask, "Hey, I just made a huge batch of soup. Did you have dinner yet?" or "I'm getting a group together to go apple-picking and make apple sauce at my house. Do you want to come?" In Cambridge, people did not visit each other unless they had been invited weeks in advance. My neighbors never knocked on my door to offer me food. When I telephoned my new acquaintances and asked how they were, they always answered, "Oh, I've been really busy," which made me shy about inviting them to do anything. To make friends out east, you had to develop a thicker skin.

It took over a year to get to know half a dozen single women I could call—one at a time—to see a movie. Even if I could find a time when everyone was free, I couldn't have gotten two of these women to see the same movie on the same night and sit in the same row. Everyone had strong opinions about what she wanted to see, what show time best suited her schedule, and how far she had to sit from the screen.

My new friends and I would go to a restaurant after the movie to talk, but most nights, every place was packed, so I started saying, "Let's just go to my place. It's quieter, and I have some food." I hadn't turned into the kind of single person who ate cereal for dinner. I always kept enough groceries in my refrigerator to make a salad and a pasta dish. In Green Bay, even Francis, the friend who couldn't cook, had offered me lunch; after our long walks at the sanctuary, the tomato soup she made out of a can and the celery she smeared with peanut butter were just the right combination of hot and cold, salty, crunchy, and gooey.

I progressed from having friends over for impromptu dinners to inviting them ahead of time. "I'll prepare something simple so it won't be any trouble," I said. The following year, I started having two or three guests over for a more elaborate dinner—an appetizer, an entree, bread, salad, pie. Then I threw birthday and book publication parties for my new friends. By moving the furniture, putting pillows on the floor, and baking a couple of homemade pizzas, I could entertain as many as twenty people in the one room that was my living room, dining room, and bedroom. The guest list, compiled by the author or the birthday person, sometimes included people I didn't know. When the party was at my place, the part I dreaded—explaining who I was and why I was there—was suddenly no problem.

My new friends in Cambridge were writers, and except at parties, I saw them one at a time. None of them ever asked me what I was writing and how it was going. After staring at the same sentences for hours, erasing and rearranging them and wondering what they even meant, it was a relief to go out to a movie with someone who had spent a day doing the same thing and didn't want to talk about it. I didn't have to explain why I was so often dazed and inattentive. On the rare occasions when we did discuss our work, we weren't just making small talk or comparing notes. We were confiding in each other about what mattered the most.

IN ENTERTAINING, as well as in knitting, I had gradually moved from the easy, casual format to the more elaborate. The salad and pasta dinner after the movie was as simple as the seamless sweaters I used to knit, and just as fail-safe. When I said that I had food at my house anyway, or that I would make something simple so it would be no trouble, I was reassuring myself more than my guests and keeping the pressure low. I had gotten a job at Harvard by telling myself that the interview was a practice run. No matter what I was doing, I became terrified of bad luck when I openly wished for too much. Unlike my grandmother, though, I wasn't really content with less, or so much less.

The one subject in which I didn't mind taking tests in high school and college had been history. I loved reading about the kings and the queens, the reformers and the crooks, the new countries that appeared on the map of the world only to disappear by the following day's lecture, but I had such difficulty with dates and other small details that I stopped trying to memorize them. At the midterm or the final, I skipped the objective part and concentrated on the essay questions. I usually managed to write my way around the details I couldn't recall. When my answer was halfway between right and wrong, it was especially important to place only the right details where they stood out. I enjoyed navigating through those essays; years later, when I improvised around the mistakes I made in knitting or adjusted the pattern to accommodate my uneven hand-spun yarn, I felt the same sly satisfaction.

I suffered nosebleed and migraines at the math test, because I couldn't remember which was sign or cosign, and I panicked at English tests, because the perfect answers I knew couldn't be put on paper in the allotted time. History was the one subject in which I wasn't either good or bad. The B I got was exactly what I deserved. Long after I finished school, I continued to read history books. I forgot the details even as I was turning the pages, but I understood the overall story.

No matter where I taught, I wanted my students to relax and enjoy what they could, the way I had lucked into appreciating history. But being a teacher was like being one of the three spinners doling out every mortal's fate—only, it was talent instead of life span I was called upon to judge. My new students at Harvard impressed me with their intelligence, their knowledge of the world, and their willingness to work hard. Many were good writers and a few seemed truly gifted. All of them would have been better off if I could have persuaded them to expect a little less.

The essays they composed about their junior year abroad were full of lively details and sophisticated cultural observations, but the true story lay in the disappointment of rooming with another American student whose politics embarrassed them or the frustration of having a brother or a sister visit during the worst week of their stay. These small and yet troubling experiences—mentioned in passing—hinted at complications that revealed their personal quirks and family histories, but I could seldom convince the students to pursue the stories they considered so trivial. The few who focused on pain wrote about the depression, anorexia, or sexual abuse they had suffered. Asked to stand back and provide more perspective—or else return to the topic when they were ready to do so—they gave me revisions in which the huge unmitigated pain was described in even more detail and with less perspective.

In one of my classes, a young woman workshopped an essay about the discrimination she suffered for being a full-figured black contestant at a beauty pageant where all the others were white and several dress sizes smaller. The upshot of her story was that—due to the judges' racially-skewed notion of beauty—she was chosen as a runner-up instead of being crowned the overall winner she deserved to be. In the class discussion, it came out that there had been thirty contestants rather than the four or five that the essay seemed to imply.

"You mean there were twenty-eight people who didn't win any awards?" I asked.

The writer nodded.

"Maybe you should make that clearer. That changes the story completely."

"Why?" one of her classmates asked. "She didn't win. What difference does it make, how many other people also didn't?"

"If I was in a contest with thirty people instead of five and I came in second," I said, "I'd be thinking, Wow, I did pretty well. I almost won. I should be proud of myself. Better luck next time."

To my surprise, no one laughed. The room was quiet for a long time. Finally, one of the men said, "Okay, maybe you have a point there. But more importantly, a beauty pageant isn't a venue known for racial fairness, so the writer needs to explain why she expected to win."

My remark—that finishing second out of thirty wasn't so bad—was forgotten in the discussion that followed.

The student worked hard on her revision. After she provided more background and polished her sentences, her frustration with the "racial discrimination" came across even more dramatically. She would have been better off if the essay had fallen apart in the revision, forcing her to start over from scratch or write something else. The true story of the pageant was about her feeling more insulted by her runner-up status than with no placement at all. Just how big a part race played in her disappointment was an interesting question, but to really tell that story, a semester wasn't long enough. In the few weeks she had left, she would only have gotten to a third or fourth draft that looked worse than the first. A beginning student often has to choose between finishing a bad piece and starting a good piece that might get worse and worse before it began to improve. I had been a more effective teacher for those Midwestern kids who had been getting B's and C's through school. For them, imperfection was a fact of life. I didn't know how to get a group of sophisticated high-achievers to value a bad good story over a good bad story.

STAYING IN GREEN BAY had kept me from admitting how narrow my life was becoming. In the small towns and suburbs of the Midwest, it was a virtue not to expect too much or to stand out. If you had more money or education than your neighbors, you played down the difference until you no longer noticed it yourself. Having grown up in Japan as a girl, I had found it quite easy not to appear more accomplished than anyone. If I didn't move away, I might have grown unable to distinguish modesty from mediocrity. I had to move to Cambridge and force myself to live among more ambitious people.

But once settled there, I became more uncomfortable than ever with the competitive notion of excellence. It was exhausting to be around students who wanted to be the best at everything— even a beauty pageant they believed to be rigged. I preferred making mistakes and trying activities I could never excel at. Even my five-day condo purchase, which impressed my new friends, hadn't been perfect. I learned about real estate by reading *Home-buying for Dummies* and ignored half the advice the book offered, starting with the huge math worksheet in the first chapter that was the foundation of all the other advice because it determined how big a mortgage I could really afford. I calculated my price range from the down payment I had, and instead of getting three mortgage quotes, I went with the mortgage broker who shared Pebble's office so I wouldn't have to find a ride to another part of town. I had planned my apartment hunt the way I approached a weaving project, with an overall plan of action broken down into steps and stages, but in practice, I improvised and fudged the way I did in my knitting even when I was following a pattern. I could only be good at something if no one expected me to be perfect. Living in Cambridge, where few people had time for old-fashioned home-making, I devoted myself to cooking and knitting.

In the middle of Harvard Square, I found a small yarn store with plastic milk cartons of yarn crammed against every wall and shawls and sweaters hanging from the ceiling on invisible wires. The women who worked there were dressed in the sweaters they'd made. Customers sat at the table in the middle of the cluttered room, getting a private lesson or just hanging out to work on their projects. The store ladies and the customers alike commented on the yarn I was buying or the sweater I was wearing and told me what they had made from the same yarn. Unlike anywhere else in my neighborhood, I was free to talk to strangers without being introduced first, or needing to exchange phone numbers and email addresses at the end. This was another thing I'd been missing: casual, no-big-deal contact with people I might or might not see again. I had spent the first few months in Cambridge believing that I had offended the couple who ran the corner grocery store because they never asked me if I was new in town, where I'd moved from, or what I was going to make with the huge bag of peaches I bought. At first I liked not being stared at, but after a while, I was "creeped out," as Chuck would say, by the way people in my new town stared straight ahead and made no comments about the weather or the earliness of the hour as we stood side by side waiting for the same train. The yarn store, where women gathered around the table surrounded by bright colors and chatted about their needlework, felt like a shrine to warmth and civility.

I knitted every night at home, making sweaters from patterns that had two-page instructions in tiny print. In my twenties and thirties, I had wanted everything I did to express what I considered my essential nature: casual, relaxed, and intuitively creative, rather than formal, precise, and meticulous. Now, in my forties, I was finally ready for balance. If following step-by-step instruction didn't come naturally to me, that was all the more reason to try it. I would rather knit from a complicated pattern and make a few mistakes than execute an easier one flawlessly. A bad good sweater deserved my time and effort much more than a good bad one.

The folklore among knitters is that everything hand-made should have at least one mistake so an evil spirit would not become trapped in the maze of perfect stitches. A missed increase or decrease, a crooked seam, a place where the tension is uneven—the mistake is a crack left open to let in the light. The evil spirit I wanted to usher out of my knitting and my life was at once a spirit of laziness and of over achieving: that little voice in my head that whispered, I won't even try this, because it doesn't come naturally to me and I won't be very good at it.

THE HARDEST THING I MADE in Cambridge was a pair of mittens called "Flip-Flop Mittens," whose top half could be made to flip back like a hinged lid, exposing the fingers in a fingerless glove. I thought of them as "cat mittens": at the necessary moment, the sheath pulled back and out came the claws. It was a slow and complicated project. To achieve the gauge for the pattern, I had to use number zero needles. The new bamboo set I bought in the Harvard Square store resembled long toothpicks. The fuzzy mohair yarn made the stitches difficult to see, and each finger had to be knitted separately. It took me two months to make myself a pair. Then I started another pair for my friend Junko, whose hands were smaller than the smallest measurement in the directions. I was proud of having managed to follow the directions and, at the same time, make a few adjustments on my own, until I finished the second mitten and realized that—only on that hand—I had caused the top to flip forward instead of back. After thirty years, I had been blown back into the purgatory of mismatched hands. Once again, I was defeated by the mitten, the ultimate symbol of home-making.

The next morning, I sat down and thought of the various tricks I'd learned in my years of knitting. I looked at several knitting books, went over the notes I'd made in the margins of some patterns. Finally I figured out how to snip one stitch on the palm, unravel a few rows around it to detach the flip at the front, make a new edging for it, and graft the stitches to the back of the hand so that the flip now faced the correct way. The procedure left a small scar, hardly noticeable in the fuzzy mohair. When I gave the mittens to Junko, I showed her my mistake. Across the back of her left hand stretched a broken line, like a rural road on a map of the desert, a path across unknown terrain.

The Knitting Notebook

T HE SPECKLED BLACK "COMPOSITION" BOOK in my knitting bag has a record of every project from the last fifteen years—what I was making, which yarn I used, the number of skeins, the needle size, the gauge, the final measurements. This information only takes a few lines, so most of the space is filled with the scratch marks I made: for every five rows I knitted, I drew four vertical lines with a diagonal slash across them. The tally resembles bundles of kindling stacked across the page.

I'd been knitting for nine years before I made the shawl on the first page for my friend Jane's birthday. I can't remember what happened to the earlier notes. Even from this notebook, I only have vague recollections of the baby blankets, sweaters, and hats for Chuck's nephews, the scarves and mittens for friends I haven't seen in years.

Because I took my knitting everywhere, the margins of the notebook are scribbled with names, telephone numbers, and addresses, directions to the bookstores where I gave readings, hotel and rental car information. Some of the names are illegible and others might refer to someone who picked me up at the airport or to an author whose book I meant to read. The notebook is a shadow journal, a record of the last fifteen years in a code I can hardly decipher. The writing in it—an assortment of facts with no commentary—is the opposite of a composition.

WHEN CHUCK CAME TO SEE ME in Cambridge during my third year there, we drove to Walden. The park was half an hour from where I lived, but I had been saving it for Chuck's visit. Rereading the book together in Milwaukee the year we met, we had pictured Thoreau sitting by a shallow pond and gazing at lily pads like a New England Buddha. Actually, Walden was a freshwater lake so vast and deep that we were afraid to swim in it. We hiked around its perimeter and came across the site of Thoreau's cottage, marked by a pile of fist-sized rocks. A sign explained that people had brought these rocks from all over the world to pay tribute, even though the original structure had been made of wood.

Everyday for a week, I planned an outing so Chuck could meet the friends I'd made. Patricia, the woman who'd introduced me to her realtor, Pebble, had us over to dinner, and another close friend and novelist, Mako, went with us to an outdoor sculpture park in the suburbs. I organized a "Meet Chuck" pizza party for a dozen others. Chuck and I saw more people and sights in a week than we had done in several years of our marriage. He told funny stories about the first- and second-graders he taught, the middle-aged football league he had joined, the times Dorian had terrorized people who came to our house.

At the end of the visit, as we waited for his plane at Logan, we talked about how I would find another job in the Midwest, build a cottage in Door County, and we would visit each other every summer. Two years later, I applied to over fifty jobs, hoping to move back to the Midwest, but the best offer I got was in Northern Virginia. I moved to a co-op apartment in DC, two subway stops from Dupont Circle, where Chuck and I had stayed in the 1980s. My new running routes overlapped those we'd done from our hotel. When I called to give him my new address, Chuck said he might be getting married.

"How do you mean, might?" I asked.

"Well, I haven't decided," he answered. "I could see getting married to this woman, or selling the house and moving out to the country by myself."

"How long have you been seeing her?"

"Two years, off and on."

"If you were to get married, when would that be?"

"Oh," he said, "probably in a couple of weeks."

"Good luck making a decision," I said, and he actually laughed.

For the first time since our divorce, he didn't mention visiting me in Door County someday. As we were saying goodbye, I remembered how, every night after dinner during his stay in Cambridge, he had gone up to the roof of my condo. I had assumed he was smoking or needing to be alone, so I didn't ask what he was doing. He would come down while I was making coffee, and we would stay up talking about books and movies and mutual friends before I went to sleep in my writing room, giving him the bed as I did to any other guest. At the time, none of this had seemed strange or even particularly sad. I'd been delighted to be friends with him still, to be able to share the life I'd made out east. But now I imagined him standing alone on that roof with the skyline of Boston in the distance, the maple leaves rustling around him. How he must have felt about being a visitor in the home I'd made without him—in the long hours we talked, we could never broach that conversation.

Because he didn't call again, I wasn't surprised to hear that he had gotten married, though not even his sisters could say when or where. He emailed me on my birthday and explained he couldn't telephone this year because his wife wasn't—yet—comfortable with his being friends with me. Every year of our acquaintance, he had sung me a loud and off-key rendition of "Happy Birthday," which was even better after I'd moved away, because, on the phone, he could really ham it up and we weren't afraid to say how much we enjoyed being in touch with each other. I pictured the pile of rocks where Thoreau's wooden cottage used to be and wondered about the hundreds of people who had brought them. Dedicated readers of the book, they must have known that the original shack wouldn't have had any stones. Sometimes, the ritual didn't match the past it was meant to honor, but it was no less real for that. The rocks told their own story.

 ⁀

I WENT BACK TO GREEN BAY a year later to give a talk at my former college. Jim, the Black Sheep priest, drove me to see my old house, which was being rented out. Chuck and his new wife had bought a house in another part of town. I hadn't heard from him, but his sister, Carrie, came to DC on business and stayed with me.

The house was newly painted, and the tenants had taken down our blinds and put up white curtains. As Jim and I walked up the empty driveway into the back yard, we remembered the afternoons we'd spent with the waxwings and the robins inside the walk-in cage that used to be under the maple trees, when I was working as a sanctuary volunteer. To help the birds figure out how to forage, I had buried earthworms in clay planters and tied grapes onto branches hung from the cage's ceiling. Once the birds were eating on their own, I released them in my yard, but one robin kept returning—landing at my feet every time I went outside, rubbing his wings and opening his beak to beg for food. From the top branch of our tallest maple, that robin could tell me apart from other humans. He showed no interest in anyone else who came into the yard, but as soon as I stepped out the door, he flew down, making a huge commotion of chirps, trills, and squawks. In September as the birds began to flock up for migration, I watched my robin from inside the house, through binoculars. When he came down from the tree and didn't see me, his head bobbed down into the grass to peck at the insects. So I started ignoring him no matter how he loudly he begged. After a week, he stopped flying down to visit me and disappeared from his perch on the maple. If he was still in the yard, I couldn't tell him apart from the others. I didn't know for certain if he had survived to join the flock. This was the saddest event in my years as a volunteer rehabilitator. I told Chuck how great it felt to do the right thing and let that bird go, and he pretended, for my sake, that this was the whole truth.

Jim and I crossed the back yard and came around to the east side of the house. As we proceeded along the narrow side garden, we were only a few feet away from the house, so the scratches and the gouges on the old paint were impossible to miss. It was April, too early for Chuck to be working outside. He must have started the previous fall and run out of time before the tenants moved in or the cold weather set in. The scratches might as well have been a hieroglyphic message. I had emailed him from DC and asked him to call my cell phone during the two days I would be in Green Bay. We could meet for coffee or at least talk on the phone. If that wasn't possible, I said, he could tell me so by email and I would understand. Though he didn't respond, I knew what he was thinking: *I should call her soon. I just haven't gotten around to it yet.* A person who doesn't finish anything will never write you off, either. As long as we're both alive, he must be hoping, there is still a possibility we would be friends again.

WHILE I WAS STILL LIVING IN WISCONSIN, my brother had telephoned me from various airports around the U. S. Sometimes, he was changing planes between South America and Japan and other times, he had stopped in New York or California to visit friends.

"Next time," he always said, "I'll come to Green Bay."

In the background, I could hear the noise of the terminal. If he had really wanted to talk, Jumpei wouldn't have waited until the last few minutes he was in the country to call me. He didn't fully understand how his actions had betrayed me. He might even have been hoping that his various loyalties could co-exist—his travels in South America, his closeness to Michiko, his business in Tokyo, his friends in the U. S., and me, his only blood relative. Like a needle working its way through an intarsia sweater, he wanted to be immersed in each block of color, one at a time. I should have understood that desire more than anyone, but when he finally stopped calling, I was relieved.

I haven't been in touch with anyone in Japan since then. My grandmother, Fuku, died a year after our only visit; my two favorite aunts, Akiko and Keiko, too, a few years later from cancer. The last time I saw the uncles, aunts, cousins, and friends I still have, my novel had gotten translated into Japanese, and the publisher had arranged a book tour in Tokyo and Kobe. My relatives and friends took me out to dinner, and I promised to stay in touch, but once I was back in Wisconsin, I only thought, as Chuck would do about me later, *I should write soon, I just haven't done it yet*. None of my female cousins or close friends had ever worked full-time. My two uncles who are teachers don't have women colleagues or friends. The last woman they regarded as their equal was probably my mother, who they always said was the smartest of my grandparents' children. My relatives and I have little in common anymore; even if we'd lived in the same country, we might have fallen out of touch. All the same, letting go is as scary as making contact, so I balance in the middle, postponing my decision indefinitely.

My mother had no use for indecision. In her journal, she never weighed the value of life against the relief she sought in death. She mentioned a few things she thought she *should be* grateful for—my brother and me, the home she'd made, the family she came from—but that's not the same as finding joy in us and feeling grief at the thought of losing us. When she imagined her only alternative, she quickly ruled it out: death seemed far less painful to her than leaving her husband and going back alone to her parents' house. In every entry, she made a list of things that depressed her, the reasons why she shouldn't be alive. For the two years she wrote, Takako never wavered: she was gathering evidence against her life and nurturing her resolution. Once she became sure, she planned her suicide so carefully that there was no possibility of being brought back to life. When she insisted that my father take my brother and me on a rare Sunday outing, she was making sure that we would not be alone to find her. She thought of every detail and never wondered if she was making the right choice. If she had left her marriage instead, her parents could have loved and consoled her as she endured her disgrace; my brother and I might have come to her when we were old enough to leave our father's house. Even if we didn't, she wasn't going to lose us any more in life than in death, but she wasn't thinking of these chances. Takako didn't believe in God or afterlife. She chose the absolute certainty of death—pure nothing—over the banal compromises of life.

Because I've spent most of my life in the shadow of her suicide, I'm drawn to compromises and ambiguity. I stayed in Green Bay for years pondering the changes I could be making. Indecision struck me as a kind of freedom, a chance to draw out every potential action into a long yarn of what might have been and could still be. Even the most complicated sweaters are made of loops of yarn. You can snip one stitch to unravel the whole sweater and start over indefinitely, making several sweaters out of the same yarn and never having to stop. Compared to what my mother had done—choosing the ultimate change, which was death—staying in one place and making no progress seemed like safety and contentment. But when Chuck started doing the same thing with our house, starting and stopping but never finishing, I could no longer live with him. Making no decision didn't protect me from change. Things ended whether I finished them or not.

I've un-knitted necklines that looked sloppy or cuffs that turned out too tight and replaced them. There were a few sweaters I took apart around the halfway mark, because I didn't like the way they looked, and no amount of adjusting could save them. But in all the years of knitting, I have never unraveled a whole finished sweater and knitted it into a new garment. Though nothing I've made is perfect, after numerous partial corrections, there comes a time to accept the result and move on to something new. The pleasure of knitting and unraveling, finishing nothing, is potent. Sometimes, I imagine myself sitting in a magic circle of invisible stitches, endlessly repeating the same easy motion. But I have a notebook full of scratch marks to remind me of the stitches I've made and kept.

Notes for Further Reading and Knitting

BOOKS THAT TAUGHT ME HOW TO KNIT:

Fee, Jacqueline. *The Sweater Workshop*. Loveland, Colorado: Interweave Press, 1983.

This book introduced me to the seamless sweater and the watchcap (which Fee calls "the mushroom cap"). "Candle-Lit Windows," the pattern I put in the yoke of Chuck's pullover, also comes from this book.

Zimmermann, Elizabeth. *Knitting Without Tears*. New York: Scribners, 1971.

The tam-o'shanters I made with Katie and the cardigan (cut open from a pullover) that I didn't try are both in this book. Zimmermann's chapter on hats includes watchcaps and "snail hats."

———. *Knitter's Almanac*. New York: Scribners, 1974.

Zimmermann introduces a new project for each month. The shawl I knitted for Alice is for July. Zimmermann made hers while accompanying her husband on his business trip to Europe.

OTHER KNITTING BOOKS:

Carles, Julie and Jordana Jacobs. *The Yarn Girls' Guide to Simple Knits*. New York: Clarkson Potter, 2002.

———. *The Yarn Girls' Guide to Beyond the Basics*. New York: Potter Craft, 2005.

Fassett, Kaffe. *Glorious Knits*. New York: Clarkson Potter, 1985.

Fourgner, Dave. *The Manly Art of Knitting*. Santa Rosa, California: Threshold, 1972.

"Only a man would knit a hammock with shovel handles and manila rope for yarn," according to the back cover.

Galeskas, Beverly. *Felted Knits*. Loveland, Colorado: Interweave Press, 2003.

Ligon, Linda (Ed). *Homespun Handknit: Caps Socks Mittens & Gloves*. Loveland, Colorado: Interweave Press, 1987.

Walker, Barbara. *A Treasury of Knitting Patterns*. New York: Scribners, 1968.

Barbara Walker collected 107 traditional lace patterns for this book.

PATTERNS I USED:

The felted bowler was made from "Fabulous Felted Hat" designed by Rena Brown and Carol Dunlap, published by Brown Sheep Company. Similar patterns appear in Beverly Galeskas' *Felted Knits*.

"Sweater Sweater" was designed by Norma Jean Ek.

The pattern for "Flip-Flop Mittens" appears in a pamphlet, *Mittens, Gloves, Hats, and Scarves* (Lowell, Massachusetts: Classic Elite Yarns, 2000).

"Emmeline" (my first cardigan) can be found in *Rowan Knitting Magazine, Number 28*.

THE GENERAL HISTORY OF KNITTING, WEAVING AND SPINNING:

Barber, Elizabeth Wayland. *Women's Work: The First 20,000 Years*. New York: Norton, 1994.

Macdonald, Anne. *No Idle Hands: The Social History of American Knitting*. New York: Ballantine, 1988.

Rutt, Richard. *The History of Hand Knitting*. London: B. T. Batsfold, 1987.

THE HISTORY OF MULTI-COLORED KNITTING IN THE BALTICS:

Bush, Nancy. *Folk Socks: The History and Techniques of Handknitted Footwear*. Loveland, Colorado: Interweave Press, 1994.

De Masters, Sandy and Mary Germain. *Ethnic Socks and Stockings*. Copyright, De Masters and Germain, 2002. This booklet was compiled for the class the authors taught at Sievers School on Washington Island, Wisconsin.

Upitis, Lizbeth. *Latvian Mittens*. Pittsville, Wisconsin: School House Press, 1997.

COCO CHANEL:

Charles-Roux, Edmonde. *Chanel and Her World: Friends, Fashion, and Fame*. New York: The Vendome Press, 2005.

Special thanks to Sabina, wherever you are, for teaching me to knit.

Kyoko Mori

K yoko Mori's award-winning first novel, *Shizuko's Daughter*, was hailed by the *New York Times* as "a jewel of a book, one of those rarities that shine out only a few times in a generation." Her many critically acclaimed books include *Polite Lies, The Dream of Water*, and the novels, *Stone Field, True Arrow* and *One Bird*. Her stories and essays have appeared in *The American Scholar, The Kenyon Review, The Prairie Schooner, Harvard Review, The Best American Essays*, and other journals and anthologies. Mori holds a Ph.D. in English/Creative Writing from the University of Wisconsin-Milwaukee. She was Briggs-Copeland Lecturer in Creative Writing, Harvard (1999–2005) and, for the last 5 years, on the faculty of the Lesley University Low-Residency MFA program in Cambridge. Kyoko Mori is associate professor of English at George Mason University. She lives in Washington, DC with Ernest and Algernon—her Siamese cats.